COURAGE IS MY CROWN

UZMA PINKS ZAMIR

authors
AND CO.

Disclaimer:

The authors have tried to recreate events, locales and conversations from their memories of them. In order to maintain their anonymity in some instances they have changed the names of individuals and places, they may have changed some identifying characteristics and details such as physical properties, occupations and places of residence.

CONTENTS

1

THE OCEAN OF GRIEF

$\mathcal{L}$ et me start with congratulating you for taking the time to read this book and be inspired by the incredible Muslim women who will be sharing their courageous journeys.

When I had the idea for Courage is my Crown I wanted something specifically tailored to Muslim women for them to feel inspired, to gain knowledge, tap into their own inner power and to know they are enough, and I am so glad you are on this journey with us.

We women are incredibly courageous. It's a gift given to us by our Lord that naturally allows us to dig deep and find strength when faced with the toughest situations. We hold so many roles in such an effortless way that we can forget how amazing we are at times playing the role of the caring daughter, the loving mum and the aunty who protects like a mother and bonds like a friend.

As Muslim women we complete half of our faith on the day we become a wife and we naturally go on to love our new family like our own.

There are also going to be times when we will go through life with a broken heart and bleeding with pain, yet our crown of courage and strength is firmly glued to us. I mean, seriously, look at us... we are kick-ass creatures!

Yet there is still this lingering cultural belief that women are the weaker sex – and that is exactly what is it is, a cultural belief with no meaning or value within Islam.

In some families this belief is stronger than others and for those women who have been undervalued their whole life, this book is dedicated to you and your strength, because you are enough!

Our lives are made up of tons of moments and decisions that required courage, strength and patience, and we must never forget the power that is buried inside. Sometimes we just don't know how strong we are until we are faced with our worst fear.

When I planned to share my journey of courage with you

I was going to talk about my journey as a Muslim

entrepreneur but, if I am honest with everyone reading this, the one thing that took every ounce of courage was losing my father. For all those sisters who are grieving for their loved ones I hope that me sharing my story helps you.

Death is something that is promised to us all regardless of faith, gender or age, yet the thought of losing someone we love is the most soul-destroying thought: this was me. The thought alone of losing my father made me weep and tore my heart into pieces.

He was my best friend, my mentor, my teacher and the man I loved with every ounce of my heart, and if I knew anything, it was that living without my dad was simply impossible.

As a Muslim when someone leaves this temporary world we call our home we are taught to recite the following:

Inna lillahi wa inna ilayhi raji'un, which is part of a verse from the Qur'an which translates to, "We belong to Allah and to Allah we shall return." Reciting this verse for the man who raised me was the moment my heart broke.

I wish I could share everything with you in this chapter but even fifteen months on, my mind and heart don't understand how I have survived this heartache. Grief for me was an emotion that isolated me from so many, some of them my closest friends, and connected me with strangers.

The effort of trying to explain how I was feeling in that dark hole was just exhausting, and I found myself not even wanting to talk to anyone who hadn't experienced the same loss. My grief gave me two different personalities and identities, which is simply mind boggling for the soul.

There was one side of me who would weep, cry, scream and simply couldn't come to terms with my loss, and the other side of me was the one people expected to see. Coping well (whatever that is), back on social media, starting work again and doing all the normal things like it was something I could just snap back from.

Losing a loved one is a life changing event and don't ever let anyone dictate how you should be grieving. It can be a very lonely journey even if you are sharing that loss with your family.

When I look back at all the conversations I was having within days of losing my dad, all the words which were meant to be words of comfort to me felt like empty words. People were telling me it was going to be okay and time would be a healer and all I wanted to do was scream in their faces.

I wish I could share the depth of my grief with you in this chapter. I am sure many in the same boat could relate to every word, yet there are so many things my heart just isn't ready to share. However, I hope to leave you with some drops of courage.

My Grief changed me, my life, my identity and my view on absolutely everything. For those of you who have experienced something similar you may feel the same and I want you to know it's okay. I remember living in the same three outfits for over four months, I hated looking at my wardrobe.

That wardrobe was full of character and colour – something that was no longer present in my life. I didn't take any selfies, didn't socialise, didn't wear make up for absolutely months, things that I didn't even think twice about before. I just didn't have it in my heart to do them any more because everything was so damn dull.

I remember sitting in front of my big mirrors and asking myself, Who are you Uzma? It was like I had no ambition, no courage, no desire to achieve anything. I felt empty. I looked in the mirror and saw a broken woman where once I had seen a strong Muslim woman who pushed to be a role model for others.

I had been an entrepreneur, passionate about helping

other people, someone who wanted to create change for women and leave a legacy, but now there was nothing. It was like the person who I once was had been buried six foot under and the more I tried to chase her the more tired I got, and that right there was the issue. It was like there was an invisible pressure to be "ok" and the old me again for others.

My friends on social media missed my inspirational and motivational posts while I just about managing to get out of bed. When any life changing event happens it's normal for it to have a knock-on effect in other areas of your life, so this is your reminder to focus on you and only you.

Having a huge amount of pressure to feel or act in a certain way is not going to serve you in any way. As women it's our natural instinct to put others first but on a journey of grief or hardship we must learn to soothe our aching heart in any way we feel is right for us.

What may provide comfort to one doesn't have to be the same method you must adopt, so don't ever feel you need to apologise for your actions or act in a way that pleases society.

Imagine you are running a five mile race and you can see the finish line but when you are minutes away it is extended by another mile. You take a deep breath and run another mile. Once again when it is within touching distance it's moved again by another two miles. You dig deep and take your exhausted body to the new finish line and once again just before you reach the end it has been moved again.

Jeez... just writing that made me feel tired! This is the exact same scenario as when you try living your life by other people's expectations. You will get pulled in different directions, none of which will serve you.

This was something my dad taught me from a young age: never live to please other people because you won't find happiness or peace.

I want to share a number of teachings I was taught by dad that Inshallah will give you guidance and strength in any hardship.

"Verily, with every hardship comes ease!"

- 94:6 Quran

This quote is one of my favourite teachings. Having a light at the end of the tunnel can become a glimmer of hope that guides us out of a dark tunnel. My dad always taught me to have faith in my Lord and that he is the greatest of planners.

Choosing to count your gratitudes and know that things will get better can help in retraining our mind to subconsciously believe things will get better. As the famous quote goes, if you believe it will happen then you are halfway there.

Believe in yourself.

Self-belief is one of the biggest gifts my father gave to me. I was always taught to trust my own gut instinct and believe in my own strength and this was a huge game changer. I always sought knowledge and guidance, but I never allowed anyone to dictate what they thought I could or couldn't do.

My self-belief is my power and the key firmly stayed in my hand. This played a huge part when I decided to start my first business at twenty one with no experience. I was told by many I wouldn't be able to succeed but the voice of my dad telling me I could was much louder than any other voice.

So, if you ever find yourself doubting yourself or listening to that negative voice, ask yourself whose voice that is. In most cases it's someone who didn't have the best influence on us. Once you have identified that then ask yourself whose voice you will choose to listen to, the one that empowers you or the one which disempowers you.

Choose to feed your mind with love, self-belief, kindness and tons of encouragement as it will always over-power the negativity fed to you by others.

"Verily, only the believer will be shaded on the Day of Resurrection in the shade of his charity."

- Quran

A huge teaching from my father was to be honest and a good person in this world so it would be our acts of charity in the next. Finding comfort in giving back to others is something that truly allowed me to find a meaning for my life in my difficult times.

My dad taught us to give to charity in any way we can but in a simple and discreet manner, so it feeds your soul not your ego. Prophet Muhammed (PBUH) once said: A man who gives in charity and hides it, such that his left hand does not know what his right hand gives, his charity will be in the shade on the Day of Judgement.

I found that when everything was dark and I questioned why I was even alive and what my purpose was in this world, looking at ways I could help others created a huge shift in my focus.

I asked myself one day what I wanted to be remembered for when I was no longer here. I wanted to leave an impact on people whereby they would raise their hands and pray for me, remember me and give to charity in my name.

I received tons of messages when I lost my father and many women reached out to remind me how blessed I was to have such an incredible bond and how many grew up without that love – the love and guidance of a father figure – and that inspired me to launch my mindset mentoring business Power Up with Pinks.

I wanted to help women find the inner power and self-belief that my dad helped me find. Without his love and guidance, I wouldn't be the woman I am today. If you are going through a difficult time I urge you to get involved in activities that let you give back and serve others.

Always do the right thing because your Lord is watching.

I remember being around ten and going out with my dad. We were at traffic lights when a beautiful brand new black BMW stopped next to us. Let's rewind back to the 90's when you didn't see luxurious cars everywhere. I remember turning to my dad and saying, "Wow, look at that car," and I will never forget his response.

He turned around and said, "If he has worked hard and earned his money the halal way then may God bless him with more. If he has earned it via wrong doings and harming people then the materialistic items just aren't worth it." I just remember being taken aback with dad's answer and thinking, wow, what a wise man!

The moral of the story has stuck with me my whole life. If you are grieving, a task I urge you to do is get a fresh notebook and document all the incredible things your loved one taught you, your favourite memories, the best moment and even write all your dreams down. It was like my safe box of memories so I would never forget any of my incredible moments.

Grief is an inevitable fact of life, a test that each person must at some point unfortunately go through.

Allah SWT says in Surah Al-Baqarah, verse 155, "And We will surely test you with something of fear and hunger and a loss of wealth and lives and fruits...".

As long as you are on this earth, you will likely experience a loss of someone close to you. The thought of that alone used to tear me apart. I remember crying to sleep every New Year's Eve and praying, God just give me one more year with my dad.

Bless him health and give him my life. I just didn't want any harm to come to my dad.

The fear used to paralyse me every time he was unwell or in hospital and I guess only those who have lived their worst fear day and night know the shattering pain of it becoming a reality.

I'm not going to tell you that life will ever be the same again. Our grief will stay with us until we reunite with our loved ones.

I pray you find peace and blessed with Sabr.

I pray you find comfort in the time you spent with your loved ones and cherish your memories.

I pray you can look back at photos and smile more than you cry.

I pray you find a way to grieve and express your feelings in a way that is right for you.

There is a quote, author unknown, and it goes like this,

"Grief is like the ocean; it comes in waves. Sometimes

the water is calm and sometimes it's overwhelming. All we can do is learn how to swim."

I hope you learn how to swim in the drowning ocean of grief and you never forget how courageous you are.

Lots of love from a grieving daughter.

UZMA PINKS

Hello, my name is Uzma Pinks and I am a mindset mentor for Muslim women. I am incredibly passionate about helping women achieve everything their heart desires.

My mission is to help women find their own inner power. I want to help them create an indestructible self- belief and attain the mindset of a true warrior.

They can use these new found skills to move swiftly towards their own goals in life, without ever compromising on their personal beliefs and ethics.

My chapter is dedicated to my father who held my hand since I was a child and raised me as a strong woman.

Thank you for gifting me my self-belief and the courage to believe so fiercely in my goals. Without my dad's love, support and guidance my spark would never be as bright as it is. May Allah give you the highest ranks in Jannat Ul Firdous.

Love from a grateful daughter.

Contact:

Email:

Powerupwithpinks@hotmail.com

Website:

www.Powerupwithpinks.com

facebook.com/uzma.p.zamir

2

THE GRASS IS ALWAYS GREEN ON MY SIDE

The Grass is Always Green on My Side / He loves me; He loves me not.

A warm summer's afternoon. The sun is shining, filling the world around me with an abundance of radiance. A feeling of peace fills me from head to toe. As I take in the smell of the green grass the feeling of love rushes through my body.

Stretching my arms and hugging myself, I sit up. As I glance ahead, I see a daisy, its gentle white petals talking to me. I lean forward and delicately pull the daisy out from the ground. The adolescent girl within me can't resist: I gently start to pull one petal at a time. My excited voice follows, "He loves me; He loves me not. He loves me; He loves me not."

There is an excitement and nervousness rushing through my body, and my stomach churns. I can't bear to stop and then a sigh of relief as I softly pull at the last petal and shyly smile and whisper, "He loves me."

The young me always saw herself as someone who would have what I used to call a "conventional" life; finish my GSCEs at the age of sixteen, then A levels by the time I was eighteen, finish university at twenty one and marry at around the age of twenty four, once I had established the foundation of my career.

I would be married to an honest, committed and hardworking man living "happily ever after" in a lovely, but not so big house with lots of bedrooms and a beautiful green garden. I imagined I would be holding my first born at around the age of twenty six.

I would live the life of a perfect lady of leisure and homemaker and when my loving husband would return home from work he would call out down the hallway, "Honey I'm home." I would call back down the hallway, "Freshen up, dear, dinner is almost ready." I knew I always wanted three children, ideally two boys and a girl. I wanted my daughter to have "only daughter" and "only sister" syndromes, entitling her to be spoilt.

A woman's innate and natural disposition is to want to

have children. This is something as a Muslim woman I strongly believed. Why? Because the very first introduction to my Lord that I am met with in the Holy Book is "**Ar-Rahman**", to mean **The Most Merciful**.

It is then interesting to learn this name of His is derived from the word "Raham" to mean "a womb". As a Muslim woman I was created with mercy embedded in my reproductive organ from which the innate desire to be a mother came from.

My life took a very different route to the "conventional life" I had imagined for myself. Following my father's stroke in 1990 and the ongoing challenges we faced as a family due to his slowly deteriorating and progressive illness, I found myself taking on additional responsibilities within the home, and over time I had to step up in many aspects to fill the void of a son and a brother within the home.

Having come from a family of five siblings, all sisters, living in a patriarchal society, this was not easy. For me it was simple. I did not want my father, nor my mother to feel that they could not be part of a society because they had no son, or that somehow they had failed in their lives because they had no son.I started my first part time job at McDonalds at the age of sixteen, mainly working on the fillet-o'fish station, which worked out fine for me. I was too embarrassed to work on the tills and be seen by my peers in my Mac D uniform.

Let's just say McDonalds taste for fashion was nowhere near as tasty as their food. I worked weekends and late hours a couple of weekday nights from 7pm till 1am. Following weekday shifts after a late night, I would wake up in the morning and attend sixth form where I was studying for my A Levels.

After one year I moved on to work at Asda on weekends, hiding away upstairs in the staff café. The little money I earned would be shared with my parents to contribute towards the financial running of the home.

As I started studying for my A Levels, I knew I wanted to study law and go on to pursue a career in law. According to the calculation in my head at the time, it would take me two years to qualify as a solicitor, which I would go on to do after my law degree and I would be ready to marry at twenty four, just in time. A Levels were tough, but I did it and before I knew it, I was at university and so my plans were on track: brilliant.

However, into the first semester of my first year at university, I returned home on a cold evening and learntfrom my mother that we had received a repossession order from the mortgage company. We had fallen behind on the mortgage repayments. Instantly, without a second thought, I decided I would drop out of university and get a full-time job.

I knew I had to help repaying the mortgage arrears and continue with the repayments. The thought of my father losing what had been his home since 1964, and what this would do to my parents and the family, had a huge impact on me both emotionally and mentally.

Within days I was able to secure a full-time job, starting as an audio typist and two weeks later working as a legal claims handler with an insurance company. Our home continued to be our home.

A year later I went back to university and continued my studies part-time, whilst working full time. A very long six years later I went on to complete a degree in law and graduated in 2003.

By now, as the years passed, between working a full-time job and studying an intense and demanding undergraduate degree part time, I had parked up my desire to have a career in law. I started a job in a start off law firm and was doing very well.

They had offered to support me going on to study myLegal Practice Course (LPC) and also a Training Contract. I should have been excited, but I wasn't. I was

ready to get married and be that family woman I was
yearning to be. I left my job at the law firm, unsure if,
when or how I would come back to pursue a career in
law. I moved on to the next chapter of my life:
"Marriage".

It was an arranged marriage to which I consented with all
my heart and soul. Marriage was something I had always
looked forward to, fulfilling my life and my dreams of
being a wife, a homemaker, a mother to two boys and a
girl. And of course, the "honey I'm home" echoing down
the hallway in my maybe not so large and beautiful home.

I remember my first meeting with him. I came home from
work, put on a saree and went into the room where he was
sitting. I sat down opposite him, looked up at him and said
something like, "I am the son and brother to my family,
roles that I would like to continue to fulfil. At the same
time, I will be the best wife that I can be to you. If this is
something you are happy with, then I am happy." Yeah, I
know, how naïve of me to not ask him anything else so that
I could get a picture of what our life together would be like.

Hours into my marriage, life took a drastic turn. The day
after my Nikkah, the Islamic Marriage, I knew and felt in
my gut that this marriage was not going to work. I started
to walk down a road of lies and deceit. My naivety misled

me once again and I continued in the hope that it wouldn't be as bad as it seemed.

The feeling of my gut won over my naivety and around a year and a half later I had decided that I would no longer walk down this road. He wasn't a bad man; he treated me well. His intention of marriage was very different to mine and we both wanted and needed different things from a marriage.

It was impossible for us to complement and support each other in our marriage endeavours. At the age of twenty nine, I divorced.

My dream of having three children was crushed just like that. I found myself leaning towards sadness and could feel myself breaking a little at a time.

One thing I could not do was break. Why? Being a pillar of support to my father, to my mother and to my family meant that I could not and would not allow myself to break. I feared that a broken pillar would result in a catastrophic collapse.

I had to pull myself together. During the build-up to the divorce and immediately after the divorce I found myself working two jobs to make ends meet and most importantly to keep up with the mortgage payments. I could not face the possibility of another repossession order; all my sacrifices would have been lost in vain.

Just before I married, I purchased the family home from my parents. I decided to sell the house I was living in with my parents and younger sibling and move to a new home, with which would come a new start and new dreams.

I sought life coaching, which helped me to process some of my past experiences and build new and positive dreams. I found myself rebuilding my dreams, but this time as a mature woman, directed by the experience of reality as opposed to those of princess fairy tales, sold to me by the likes of Walt Disney, waiting to be rescued by a prince.

I didn't need a prince to love me, to be my hero. Once I had worked through the pain and processed and healed from the fact that the many things I had once dreamed of had been shattered, I decided that I was going to rebuild a stronger version of me. An authentic one, not one that was directed by common ways of thinking. I was going to be my own Shero.

With my divorce, my dream of being a mother had somehow come to an end. I would find myself secretly wiping tears from my face in my attempts to console myself. To end a loveless and deceitful marriage came at a high cost.

I remember I couldn't even walk through the baby clothes section of a store; I would cry. But being strong was the only choice I had. I turned to my God and asked Him to make me strong and content with not being a mother. I asked Him to help me build another dream, a dream that could not be broken by another person.

My dreams may have been broken but not my soul. So, one step at a time I started to move forward. This did not come with ease; it was no walk in the park. It required discipline and resilience. God built me back together piece by piece, a much stronger, wiser and braver version of me.

Shortly after settling into our new home, in 2008 I also started a new job. Starting as a sessional Advice Practitioner, now I am the Consultant Head of Services for this leading Charity. The job was exciting and challenging. It kept me distracted, I was in my element, applying my skills, learning, pushing myself and being recognised, valued and appreciated for my work.

I lost my father in July 2009 after his difficult battle with dementia as a result of a number of strokes. Although losing my father was not easy during his final days and moments, sitting non-stop by his bedside at the hospital is when the spiritual me began to unravel. Reflecting on the cycle of life and death I found myself feeling closer and more connected to my Lord than ever before.

My Lord may have taken my father away from me, but He replaced it with a sweet closeness to Him. I would say it was at this time that I became a more conscious Muslim woman and started to explore and learn more about Islam, a religion I was born into. Till this day I am still learning and exploring and with every discovery I am learning more about myself.

In April 2010, not long after my father's demise, I went to perform Umrah (non-mandatory lesser pilgrimage made by Muslims to Makkah), where I was met with many amazing spiritual experiences and immense closeness to my Lord.

Thereafter every year for seven consecutive years I would go to perform Umrah. I felt special because as a Muslim I believed that visiting the city of Makkah to perform Umrah is only when Allah (God) wills it for you. And of course, for my God to will this for me every year made me feel special.

Each year would bring a different experience, a different spiritual connection, an increased feeling of proximity to

God. And then April 2017 was my last performance of Umrah and visit to Makkah and the city of Madinah (these cities are often referred to as the Holy Lands). But I did not stop feeling special, despite my yearning to be in the Holy Lands. God made me feel special in a different way.

> **"Do people think that on their mere claiming 'We have attained to faith,' they will be left to themselves, and will not be put to a test?" – Surah Al-Ankabut; The Spider; Chapter 29, Verse 2; Qur'an.**

For the most part of my formative years and adult life, God was preparing me to say, "I have attained faith" in Him, and then in 2017 it was time for my "faith" in God to be tested.

By 2009, around a year into the job, I inherited the role of General Manager. The work was increasing and so the team started to grow. The following year, with the support and encouragement of my friends and my management, I returned to university and completed my LPC.

I surrounded myself with positive thinking people, those who encouraged me to do well, and those who reached their hand out to support me, help me back up and remind me what my worth and value is. Those who believed in me.

When I returned to study my LPC, I remember my Criminal Law tutor telling me that I had made it onto the course just in time. I had seven years from completing my LLB to enrol onto the LPC. He reminded me that when I failed my European Law exam during my final year on the LLB, God had a plan for me.

I had to pause and think about what he was telling me, and there it was, it started to unfold. In order to retake the exam for European Law, I did not graduate till a year later. God always knew that I was going to get divorced and return to study my LPC and recommence my journey towards becoming a solicitor.

Everything in life happens for a reason and as time passes the reasons will unfold. For me this was and will always be a milestone moment of learning the true essence of having trust and faith in God's plan. This is my go-to moment when I feel like things are not working out for me. I tell myself God has your universe, just trust and let go.

Over time I got stuck into my studies and my work, which by the way I was again studying part time, two evenings a week, whilst working full time. It was like déjà vu. As each day passed, I was moving closer to my new goals. God was helping me become content with not being a mother and placed in me a deep passion and excitement about pursuing and focusing on my work and establishing a career.

Slowly but surely my dream of becoming a mother faded. Little did I know at the time that God was making me content, because He had a different plan for me.

Fast forward to 2016, when I started working as a Trainee Solicitor part time, two days a week. I was so excited that I was finally back on track to pursuing a career in law. It was tough trying to manage my regular job alongside my training. Both were very demanding, but I was on an adrenaline rush, just how I liked it.

Life was buzzing and felt exciting. Not long now till I am admitted to the roll of solicitors, I kept telling myself and driving myself forward: October 2019, not long.

In 2017 my health started to take a turn, with suspected endometriosis, a disease that debilitated my livelihood. As much as I tried to fight it, I was being defeated by the disease.Endometriosis is a condition in which the tissue that lines the womb (endometrium) is found outside the womb, such as in the ovaries, fallopian tubes and in or around the bladder or bowel. Endometriosis mainly affects young girls and women of childbearing age.

Symptoms of endometriosis are many, including severe pain during or between periods; significantly long, heavy and irregular periods, painful bowel movements; pain in the bladder and pain during or after sex. Women report extreme fatigue and fertility may also be affected.

Misdiagnosis is very common, taking on average around 7-10 years for women to be diagnosed. An estimated

1.5 million women in the UK, and one in ten women around the world, are reported as being diagnosed with this debilitating disease.

My symptoms of endometriosis were always there, for around two decades. It was grit it and get on, so I learned to live with the pain and many symptoms of the disease. I was going back and forth to visit my GP and being seen by a number of different consultant gynaecologists across different hospitals.

I was often told by the medical professionals that my symptoms were that of a heavy period and that it was normal. And that is what I told myself, that it was normal and carried on with life.

In 2017 when my quality of life was being compromised

and I started to miss work, I revisited my GP and pushed for a diagnosis.

Being suspected as having endometriosis was not an easy thing. It was a long process that I had to go through to get a diagnosis and that in itself speaks volume about the lack of awareness on the disease not just amongst the common people but also the medical community. But that is a story for another time.

Endometriosis meant that I had a lot of difficult and painful decisions to make. It was like the world around me was crumbling down piece by piece. The symptoms of the disease forced me to give up my Training Contract because I could no longer cope with and manage the hours of work.

I was expected to be in work at 9am, but being overcome by fatigue, not being able to sleep through the nights because of constant pain, it was impossible for me to be at work for 9am. Although I was able to negotiate a late start, even getting to the office for 10am was proving impossible.

So, the sensible yet difficult decision for me to make was to give it up. Once again, I had to park up pursuing my legal career, not knowing if, when and how I would return to this. I had to do what was right for me and my health.

I was then faced with the difficult and painful decision to significantly reduce my hours of work as Consultant Head of Services. The debilitating pain and chronic fatigue made it impossible for me to physically get into the office.

By the time I had got up, showered, got ready and driven to the office, I was already exhausted making it extremely difficult for me to perform my duties at work. I was ready to come home and go back to sleep before I even walked into my office. Increasingly I found myself working from home.

Some days I would surprise myself and get lots of things done. But those were the good days and only few and far between.

Relationships with my family members became affected and eventually started to break down. Over time the world around me was falling apart, piece by piece, day by day. I felt like I was drowning deeper and deeper into an abyss, with no way back up.

The pains were always there, getting worse. One of myfriends suggested that it could possibly be that my pain threshold was reducing and that was why I was feeling the pain more. That was a possibility, but it didn't come with any consolation.

My hormones were all over the place. Most days I would behave and conduct myself in ways that I normally would not, so much so that I could not recognise who I was. I was struggling to understand why I was behaving like this. There were many factors: the imbalance of hormones, the range of treatments to try and manage the symptoms of endometriosis, from the combined pill, to the mirena coil to Zoladex, putting me into chemical menopause.

From the moment that I could feel my health deteriorating I knew one thing: I knew that I wanted my quality of life back at whatever cost. I did lots of research, spoke to endometriosis specialist consultants and to many other women who have been through the same.

The one thing that kept coming up as a long-term treatment option was a hysterectomy. Although I knew it was not a cure for endometriosis it was the option that best alleviates the debilitating and painful symptoms of endometriosis. Many women said it gave them a new lease of life, although for other women the effect was not the same.

I made the decision to have a hysterectomy and that decision did not come with ease. By now I knew I was content that I did not want to have children. God had already placed that contentment in my heart, because He was preparing me for this moment, for this decision.

He was preparing me, not to chase and pursue a career but for this moment. Many of the medical professionals and the people around me were taken aback when I said I wanted a hysterectomy. "But you don't have children. You don't have a family," is what they would say. And I would reply, "But I don't want children and I don't want a family," And I would silently whisper to myself, "because my God has already made me content."

When I realised that I may have suspected endometriosis, I didn't feel sad or start questioning why was I going through yet another trial. Or question why it was that everybody else's life was working out and people were able to achieve their goals with ease. This was my test and I had to work with it and turn my life around. I reminded myself that God was holding up my universe and I should trust in His plan and have faith.

I chose not to feel sorry for myself and compare myself by looking at what other people had. I looked at my journey, I looked at my scars, the map they were drawing for me. I am going somewhere. My road is my road and as each day passes, the destination of my journey will unfold and reveal itself to me.

On 29 March 2018 I had a laparoscopic surgery for the purpose of investigating and removing any endometriosis found. I was informed after my surgery that no endometriosis was found. I refused to accept this as I knew my body better than anyone.

The progressive symptoms had to have an explanation, without which I would not stay quiet. Symptoms that had forced my life to come to a standstill, that had once again put my legal career on hold.

I followed my instincts and two weeks after my surgery I went back to my GP and asked for a referral to a different specialist for a second opinion. I sought the opinion of an endometriosis specialist, Mr Shaheen Khazali, at St Peter's Hospital, 125 miles from where I live.

When I first met with Mr Khazali in July 2018, he looked at the images of the previously performed laparoscopy and told me that he could see endometriosis. I had been misdiagnosed. I was fuming with anger and frustration but feeling relieved that there was now an explanation for why my life was debilitated by this chronic pain.

What could have possibly led to even further deterioration of my health, consumed me with anger and frustration at the system for letting me down and letting the millions of other young girls and women affected by endometriosis down, letting us all down.

It became clear that God had chosen me. He had handpicked me to be amongst those who would speak out and advocate and fight to be heard, fight to make a difference. So that is exactly what I did. I became pro-active in raising awareness about a disease that is not only misunderstood by the common person but also by the medical community.

Within months I became an Ambassador for the charity Women With Endometriosis working closely with the team to raise awareness on endometriosis and supporting young girls and women who are suspected of, or suffer with endometriosis to get the right diagnosis, treatment and care.

Also, the discussion on endometriosis and women's gynaecological health is a monthly feature on my radio show Women's Hour with Aamilah on Unity FM 93.5, Birmingham.

In March 2019 as a guest speaker at numerous International Women's Day events I shared my journey with endometriosis raising awareness to over 200 people, mainly women. I have also started to deliverEndometriosis Awareness workshops at grassroots organisations in the community and talking about the disease to the hitherto hard to reach women.

Not everyone around me approved of my talking about endometriosis. They were not comfortable with me using words and terms like "periods" and "pain during and/or after sexual intercourse."

These are not things a Muslim woman should be talking about. Where I could see the benefits of the work I was doing, others saw what I call a "superficial" harm. For me it was simple. I didn't need their acceptance nor approval. I was not chosen by my Lord to remain muted. He knows my strengths and abilities and placed me accordingly to His plan.

I turned to my Lord and I said, My Lord I want and need this hysterectomy. And I need You to guide me and I need You to keep me strong and that is exactly what I got. I told my Lord that I believe and have faith in You, and this is what I need from You.

And He gave me exactly what I needed. He stripped me of everything and took me to the core of myself. And now He is building me back piece by piece. On 4 June 2019 my uterus was evicted. A day that many Muslims around the globe were celebrating the festival of Eid al-

Fitr. And I was given the best Eid gift ever by my Lord, a new lease of life.

Having a hysterectomy meant parting with something within me that makes me a woman, that which is "Raham" from which derives mercy. Being maternal is linked to motherhood but I no longer have that. Yet I know I am forever a mother.

I have started a project to fundraise for a drop-in centre in Dhaka, Bangladesh, which will provide a safe space for Bangladesh's street children. These children are affected by child exploitation, trafficking, abuse, prostitution and more. Many of these children are orphans.

This is a project that keeps the motherless mother within me alive. A project I plan to work on for the rest of my life. I hope to regularly visit and meet the children who are being supported in person and also to continuously fundraise for the drop-in centre and to develop other drop in centres across the different regions of Bangladesh.

Prophet Muhammad (Peace be Upon Him) said: "If Allah (God) loves a people, then He afflicts them with trials." And for sure "He loves me."

The grass is what you make it on your side. The grass is never greener on the other side. That is a misconception that encourages us to run away from our problems asopposed to embracing our problems, our difficulties, our calamities, our trials, our challenges, our fears; whatever you may choose to call it. But it is what you make it. Everything happens for a reason and as time unfolds those reasons become apparent.

We often hear or read stories of others and think **"WOW!"** In their struggles and their achievements we connect with them, we feel for them, we celebrate them, we mourn with them.

But each and every one of us has our own story within us and when we start to focus on our own story we begin to learn to celebrate our own achievements, start to recognise our own struggles, start to see the journey, start to connect to the lessons in that journey. So, find that light within and celebrate your scars just the way you would your victory.

SHAJNA AAMILAH BEGUM

Aamilah Begum, also known by many as Shajna, is a Business Consultant by profession, which she has being doing for over eleven years.

She specialises in working with small businesses and charities to strategically develop programmes and projects. Her work also includes devising fundraising strategies and fundraising.

Aamilah is a divorcee, currently lives with her mother and is the main bread winner.

She is a volunteer Radio Presenter at Unity FM 93.5, a local community radio station in Birmingham.

She presents the Women's Hour with Aamilah show. A show that focuses on discussing issues and topics that matter to women and encourages her audience to talk, listen, understand and support each other through the airwaves.

Aamilah gave up her career in law to get married in the hope of starting a family, but destiny had other plans for her.

In 2011, Aamilah went on and completed her Legal Practice Course (LPC) and shortly after started working as a Trainee Solicitor, but she was forced to give up due to health reasons.

Aamilah is an active Ambassador for the Women With Endometriosis Charity. It is a role she takes very seriously and works passionately with the team to raise awareness of the disease and provide support to young girls and women affected by endometriosis.

She organised an Endometriosis Awareness Charity dinner, the first of its kind in the UK, which was attended by the world-renowned endometriosis specialist Professor Camran Nezhat from the USA as a keynote guest speaker.

Aamilah is a strong advocate and champion for empowerment, encouragement and equality for women.

She attends numerous women empowerment events as a guest speaker to motivate and encourage women to know their self and achieve their goals. One of her favourite quotes is "You are the most important ingredient in your life."

Aamilah is currently training to be an Islamic Counsellor.

She believes this will equip her with the professional skillset and knowledge to encapsulate her passion to help others know their self and flourish.

Aamilah considers herself to be a fighter. She embraces life with trust, hope, faith and perseverance.

Contact: -

Email:

sab@aamilah.co.uk

Website:

www.aamilah.co.uk

Facebook:

https://www.facebook.com/womenshourwithaamilah/

LinkedIn:

https://www.linkedin.com/in/aamilah-begum-shajna-950218153/

YouTube:

https://www.youtube.com/channel/UCV1v3sNvTORpZ27cWx2_44g

Mixed Cloud:

https://www.mixcloud.com/aamilah_begum/

Fund Raising Page:

https://www.justgiving.com/fundraising/Aamilah-Begum?utm_source=whatsapp

facebook.com/shajna.a.begum

twitter.com/Aamilah_Begum

instagram.com/aamilah_begum

3

POST NATAL DEPRESSION. MY JOURNEY.

"The wound is the place where the Light enters you" – Rumi

She looks at me, brown eyes sparkling. She rises, using her hands to steady herself against the wall and then toddles over to me. She raises her soft doughy arms, her plump hands reaching for me, fingers stretching, curling and then stretching out again like a starfish.

I lift her up, feeling the weight of her little body against me and pull her onto my lap. She looks up at me once again and holds my gaze for a moment and then a moment longer. I blink hard and then open my eyes wide in surprise, mama, the clown.

She shrieks with joy. The sound of her laughter is delicious, so high and loud, it tinkles like a bell. She throws her head back in the type of carefree joy that only babies and infants experience and then a second later she collapses into giggles.

I lean forward to kiss her velvety soft face, her juicy cheeks so round and full, they melt into the folds of her neck and I'm rewarded for my efforts with two soft baby arms reaching around my neck, hands clasped together at the nape.

I breathe in her baby scent, and my heart swells with love. It's an amazing feeling being a mother, so much love, so much intensity. I feel so blessed. These days I feel so connected to my daughter, so in love.

I don't tend to think about the time that came before very often any more, but every now and again there are times when my mind wanders back to what happened, to the time when I lost myself.

It was a scary thing for me, being pregnant. I've always been a perfectionist. Everything has to be just so, with no room for error. It has to be controlled.

Pregnancy is a journey that takes you along. It's not something you can dictate, so yes, I was afraid but I was happy. I was looking forward to meeting our baby, our love, the new and much awaited addition to my life.

I took all the necessary precautions. I had my vitamins daily, I did baby yoga, went to all the antenatal classes. I even managed to waddle into W H Smith to get myself the classic "what to expect when you're expecting" book and I read it cover to cover, but the truth is I had no idea of what was to come. You have to in fact expect the unexpected when you're expecting.

The day that my daughter was due to arrive in this world began like any other, completely insignificant in its normalcy. I woke up late, around 11am, relishing the last few days that I would be able to have a "proper lie in" as others told me.

My waters broke, and unlike the last scare a week or so before, this time I was certain. I called the hospital who told me to come in, so I arrived an hour later with my husband.

We were excited but nervous, and I was finding it odd but magical that I wasn't in much pain. We were sent home. On the way back from the hospital my contractions started strengthening and I thought back to my earlier musings about how there was so little pain.

I can't believe I was silly enough to think that it wouldn't get worse and when I think back to this, it makes me chuckle, the naivety of being a first-time mum. Four hours later I found myself back at the hospital. I had the epidural that I had requested and settled in for the rest of the night.

I had brought a blanket from home and some books. I looked up occasionally to see my husband, his face a source of comfort. His calm, stable demeanour always made me feel so safe and secure. My mother was seated next to him, eyes closed, lips moving in prayer for me.

The room was silent and I felt at ease. Strangely enough I was being lulled to sleep by the systematic bleeping of the machines and the sound of my baby's heartbeat.

Suddenly a strange sound pierced the calm, and left it shattered. It was an alarm. Before I knew what was happening, the room was full of doctors. I tried to focus on their words and heard them say, "Heartbeat, dropping, rising, we need to get the baby out now."

I was rushed out of my little sanctuary of calm. I will never forget the look of fear on my mother's face that she was trying but failing to conceal. I was rushed towards the door and as they wheeled me past my husband, it suddenly dawned upon me that he wouldn't be coming with me. I searched his face in those few seconds as I passed him by. He looked calm on the surface but I could see the unease underneath.

My heart felt as if it had dropped into the pit of my stomach. Have you ever experienced fear? True fear, the type of fear that just saturates you, every part of your being is arrested by it. It's as though you are paralysed.

My biggest fear was having a caesarean section. I was terrified of being operated on. It's odd what the mind does in times of extreme stress. One moment I was there in the hospital corridor, and in the next my mind had wandered back to my childhood.

I was sitting on my father's lap, clutching my finger, tears hot and heavy making tracks down my cheeks and falling to their destruction, each one taking a leap from the curve of my chin. Father would inspect my minuscule injury with such seriousness and tend to it as if it were a battlefield wound. I was always afraid of blood, of getting hurt.

I snapped back to the room I was in, an operating theatre. I would be cut open with a scalpel, me who couldn't tolerate a paper cut. I was stricken with fear.

I stared up at the ceiling, hearing my teeth chatter and click against each other, the sound oddly loud in my head. I felt detached, as if this was happening to someone else, but fear was a cord that attached itself to me and I knew this was real.

It was happening to me. As I lay there, on the cold operating table, they tilted my swollen, tired body to the left. I was confused. The surgeons told me to relax, to breathe. I was alone, without the comfort of my husband. I was full of terror, too afraid to speak. I had to do this alone. It would have to be under general anaesthetic.

All I could think was, "I can't do this alone." I lay there in silence, tears pricking my eyes but they remained there, suspended. I couldn't cry, I couldn't move, I couldn't think. I saw the surgeon's face, her brows furrowed with concern. "Please," she said, "try to stay calm." I nodded, teeth still chattering against my will. I closed my eyes, crushing the tears that had formed. I felt their wetness against my skin and everything was black. All I focused on was breathing.

I found myself back in the hospital room, my husband by my side, a look of complete and utter relief on my mother's face.

The midwife explained that because the baby's heart rate had stabilised quickly when I was in the operating theatre, they had brought me back to the room to continue my plans for a natural birth. I smiled, relieved. My whole body relaxed.

Muscles I didn't even realise I had clenched suddenly

released and I felt a wave of calm come over me. This calm, however, was short lived. Soon enough, the monitors started bleeping once again in that odd frenzied way. It was not a good sign. I looked at the monitors that showed my baby's heart rate rising and then drastically falling, only to rise again a moment later.

In that instant, I made a decision. I called the midwife and asked for the surgeon. She arrived and stood at the end of my bed. I looked at her and said, "I would like to have a C-section." She looked surprised and said we could wait and monitor the heartbeat, but I insisted. I asked for them to carry out the operation but not under general anaesthetic.

I needed my husband there with me and I knew, my mother's instinct told me, my daughter was in trouble. We couldn't wait. It was odd being wheeled back in again but this time I had my rock with me, I would be strong. I would feel the fear, but I knew it would be ok. I would have to be brave for my daughter's sake.

As they operated on me, I stared into my husband's eyes, his kind, brown eyes. One, a light caramel brown and the other the colour of black coffee, with a segment of caramel in it in the shape of a slice of pie, so unique, and so special to me. I felt that as long as I looked at him, as long as I held his gaze, I would somehow get through this. He held my hand and told me I would be ok over and over.

Each time I said I was afraid, he soothed me with his reassuring words. I listened to him and tried to believe him each time he told me that everything was ok and that it would be over soon. Suddenly, his attention was diverted.

I instantly asked, "Is she here? Is she ok?" I kept my eyes on him, unable to look at my baby, I was so afraid. He stretched out his arms and a bundle appeared before me. He held her to my face, her cheek warm and as soft as down against mine.

My arms remained by my side, pinned down with fear. That was the primary emotion I felt. Intense fear that would not subside. A year later my husband told me they had reached out to place her in my arms but I was too afraid to turn and look. How sad, a special moment, lost for eternity.

Shortly after I delivered I showed signs of sepsis and indeed a blood infection raged through my body. I lost count of how many blood tests I had, of the medication I was given. I remember feeling strange, confused. Everything was a blur.

I remember my skin itching and itching like ants were

crawling beneath the surface, a common side effect they told me later of the drugs that they were pumping into my body to take away the pain and to help me fight the sepsis.

My body swelled as I fought the infection, I was no longer myself. I don't remember much of my baby from that time.

The only clear memory I have is that she latched immediately and I felt so lucky and relieved to be able to feed her. It was the only thing I could offer her. I couldn't hold her for very long, or rock her or get up to bathe her or change her.

I felt broken, like my body had failed me, as if I were some sort of strange creature, unable to do what I was meant to. A week later I was discharged. On the journey home, I wept in the car. I wasn't quite sure why. All I know is that I felt sad and afraid.

Post-natal depression (PND) hit me like a wrecking ball. I was crushed in its path. The first five months of my baby's life were spent with a fog hanging over me.

PND is like an unwanted and unhelpful guest. It came without warning and did not leave although I desperately wanted to feel normal once again and be free from its sickening company.

Everyone says having a child is the most natural thing. Midwives, friends and relatives all described feeling a "rush of love" and spoke of bonding immediately. They said it was like falling in love all over again. I did not experience this mythical, magical rush of love.

Instead, I experienced the most intense fear and confusion. I was afraid for the safety of my baby; I was filled with dread to the brim and it spilled over. I was convinced someone would take her from me, that I needed to keep her safe from everything and everyone. I felt fiercely protective over her but at the same time I felt like I was not good enough and I would never ever be good enough for her or be what she wanted or needed.

I was desperate, so desperate to be enough for her. PND stole many things from me. It also stole from my husband. It snatched away the woman that was a wife to him and left him with a stranger in a shell. I sometimes wonder what I would have done in my husband's shoes, how I would have coped if there were such drastic changes in him.

Would I have been able to support him the way he supported me? I really don't think I could have, not for lack of trying. His courage and resilience at the darkest time of my life is something I will never ever forget or cease to be grateful for.

I felt like I was a failure. I felt unworthy and that I was a bad mother. PND was a voice in my head telling me that my daughter deserved someone better than me. When she cried and I held her close, I felt that she wasn't comforted. I was afraid that I was the reason for her tears.

I isolated myself, withdrawing from friends and family. I wouldn't leave the house. I knew something was wrong but I was too afraid to acknowledge my reality. Up until this point in my life, I had dealt with all setbacks alone.

I hadn't sought help, even whilst deep in the grip of anorexia, and so I fooled myself into believing I would manage this too, somehow. I didn't need help. Except, I did need help, I did need to reach out. I did need extra support. I thought I was being brave, battling alone but in reality, I was too afraid to accept that something was terribly wrong.

Sometimes seeking help is the bravest thing you can do. It's easy to shut people out, to build walls. What is difficult is sharing your vulnerabilities for someone else to see, to speak out and say, help me, please.

I always thought that one of the most courageous things I did was to voluntarily proceed with a c-section despite my phobia of being operated on, of being cut, of bleeding. The truth is one of the most courageous things I did was to reach out and seek help for PND. I reached out to the Barberry Centre, which I had been attending during my pregnancy for issues related to eating.

Falling pregnant had been a trigger for me and I had experienced urges to restrict my food intake, a throwback to my anorexia, another problem that I had buried and not resolved. At first, during talking therapy sessions, I had attempted to hide my feelings and pretend that I was ok but at some point, I decided to tell them how I truly felt. I finally told someone my truth, how my heart was breaking every day and how heavy the burden of my guilt had become.

I told them that I felt afraid all the time. From the moment I woke up to the moment my head hit the pillow, I was afraid, worried and weary. Sleep was no escape. I had nightmares that someone was taking my daughter from me, that I could see her in the distance and I couldn't reach her. I would wake up in the night, in a cold sweat, cheeks wet with tears and bile rising in my throat in sheer panic to look over to her bedside cot just to see her angelic face, peacefully asleep, safe from all harm.

I told them I was afraid to leave my baby, even for a moment. I would spend the entire day in one room, sometimes too afraid to leave her to even use the bathroom. I would wait until my husband came home from work.

I told them that I felt like she didn't want me, and that I was desperate for her to think that I was enough. I was desperate to know that she knew I was her mother and that I loved her, I was desperate to believe that she loved me too. I wanted her to know how sorry I was that I felt I couldn't be the mother she deserved.

My mind was always full, thoughts whirling and crashing, with background noise and a constant hum and buzz of anxiety. I saw the world through a lens of sadness, guilt and sorrow. Despite feeling this way, despite seeing and experiencing so many signs, I was still in denial about my condition. I hadn't accepted that I had PND.

Post-natal depression (PND) can happen to anyone. Previous loss of a baby, or a traumatic pregnancy or birth experience can increase the likelihood of a woman experiencing PND.

There are a number of signs to look out for. It could be one or two or more of these. These are signs to look out for as listed on the NHS website.

You can see this information online at

https://www.nhs.uk/conditions/post-natal-depression/symptoms/:

- Feeling persistently sad.
- No longer enjoying things that were previously special to you.
- Trouble sleeping at night and exhaustion during the day.
- Lack of energy or feeling tired all the time.
- Feeling you are unable to look after your baby.
- Problems with concentrating and making decisions.
- Loss of appetite or increased appetite (comfort eating).
- Feeling agitated, irritable or apathetic (you "can't be bothered").
- Feelings of guilt, hopelessness or self-blame. Difficulty bonding with your baby.
- Frightening thoughts about hurting your baby. Thinking about suicide or self-harm.

These sentences that describe how women may feel whilst suffering with PND are difficult for some people to read.

They are difficult for me to read, but it is so important to acknowledge that this is something that many women experience.

I, as a Pakistani Muslim woman, found it incredibly difficult to accept that I was experiencing some of these symptoms.

Growing up we were taught not to ask for help. We were taught that we don't seek help from outside of the community. I knew intrinsically that you never show these so-called weaknesses to authorities or medical professionals.

Family are meant to help you through, and if they cannot, the community will help but never go to outsiders. I still remember my mother telling me in a deathly serious manner, "Everything you say to the doctor goes on your record forever!"

The advice my parents gave was out of love and not malice, born from a place of their own fear, the result of what the generations before had passed on to them. I still remember the sense of fear I had around telling people anything personal about myself, as if I was handing them a weapon to use against me in the future when I would least expect it.

We are taught to believe if we are suffering mentally, be it with depression, anxiety, OCD or from PND and we reveal our thoughts to a medical professional, we will be laced up in a straitjacket and locked away, that our children will be taken from us. Nothing could be further from the truth.

This notion that is sewn into the fabric of the community stops women from seeking specialist help and support. There is a significant lack of awareness and understanding about antenatal and postnatal mental health concerns in the South Asian community which has led to a deeply ingrained stigma being attached to this subject.

This stigma was the reason I never sought help even whilst being completely controlled by anorexia. I had avoided seeking help all my life until I reached a point where something finally mattered enough for me to put aside my fears of us vs them.

I was pregnant with my first child and I wanted her to have a happy, healthy mother, so I took the step of speaking to my GP who then referred me to the mother and baby unit at the Barberry Centre in Birmingham.

I managed to take this daunting but vital first step because of the unwavering support I had from my husband who works in the medical field. I trusted him enough to believe it when he told me that they wouldn't "put me on medication" or "take my baby away".

Not everyone is lucky enough to have an understanding partner or family. There is a notion that women must suffer in silence and that it is simply the way things are, it is "the norm".

Suffering in silence is not normal, and it doesn't help. In many cases where signs and symptoms of PND manifest in mothers, it is not unusual for extended relatives, in laws and in some cases even immediate family members to refuse to believe that the mother is suffering from a serious mental health concern.

They are told and indeed expected to just carry on even when the changes in their behaviour and mental state are glaringly obvious. The sad reality is that the main perpetrators of this behaviour seems to be other women. This, although uncomfortable to read, is a reality that needs to be discussed and challenged.

Comments like, "I was up on my feet cleaning three days after giving birth," or, "You're not the first to have a baby, get over it," breed ignorance and a put up and shut up attitude. Signs of exhaustion are dismissed as laziness, and changes in mood are deemed to be dramatic, rude, intentional outbursts.

This lack of empathy and understanding can result in the

decline of a woman's mental health and can lead to or exacerbate PND.

It is essential that we raise awareness of this condition in our communities, not just in the current generation of women but across the generations. Men and women should be aware of the signs and the importance of supporting women through PND.

We need to cultivate an environment where people aren't afraid to admit their struggles and take steps to seek help. This means that people like me need to shine a light on PND so that we can understand how deeply rooted this issue is within the South Asian community.

It is only when we speak our truth that we will be able to identify the gaps that need to be bridged. If you can see that someone is displaying signs of PND, be their source of support, signpost them to where they can access help. Let them know that you will be there for them, without judgement.

Sometimes we have to reach rock bottom in order to start building our way back up. Having the courage to get through a day whilst suffering with PND or any other mental health condition requires a deep internal strength.

It is a huge achievement, one that we often don't give ourselves enough credit for.

Every second spent fighting to get through a day is testimony to your strength, even though you may not feel strong. There is life after PND and I am living it. The first step to recovery is always the most daunting. It's the bravest thing you will ever do and it requires courage but every step after that will bring you closer to recovery.

My experience, though initially heart breaking and devastating, has been one with an overwhelmingly positive outcome. The staff at the Barberry Centre where I was referred were incredible.

The professionals that I had contact with treated me with so much respect and dignity, with genuine care and concern for me as an individual. From my very first conversation, I felt at ease and that I was being heard. I was supported in a way that was almost invisible in the sense that there was no disruption to my life. I was supported in a manner that made me feel comfortable and not on edge. Slowly, I started to feel better and stronger.

I had a safe space to talk about my thoughts that seemed so wrong, so unnatural, without judgement or being ridiculed or shunned and my confidentiality was respected. I was supported through my postpartum journey and with each communication the fog seemed to lift a little more.

When I had days where I felt low, I was supported with kind words and the knowledge that I could contact someone who understood the fragile state that I was in. I was taught simple breathing exercises. I was given an explanation of what was happening to me to cause me to have these thoughts and feelings, and this gave me the sense and understanding that I wasn't alone.

I was suffering from a condition but it did not have to define me: I could overcome it step by step. I was encouraged to surround myself with positivity and put myself first. I was given the tools to help myself and understand myself better so that I could continue to grow stronger independently.

I actively avoided those people and situations that caused me distress and those who did not want to acknowledge my need for privacy and understanding at such a difficult time in my life. This was integral to my recovery.

Now, my daughter is eighteen months old and I am working voluntarily with the perinatal mental health team. I attend meetings to discuss the care I received and the impact that this had on me.

I was involved in a meeting with the Care Quality Commission and was able to talk about my experience with the service. Recently, I attended a meeting to look over and give my input into a new programme which will aim to support the positive engagement and enjoyment of the role of motherhood.

I have developed so much empathy towards mothers, be they new moms or mothers with two, three, or more children. I've discovered a passion for helping other women who are suffering with postnatal mental health concerns.

I have set up a Facebook support group for life after post-natal depression, with a focus on the issues that women face when suffering with PND and living within the South Asian community.

I'm hoping that I can be the change that I want to see. I want to raise awareness of how we as a community of mothers, fathers, brothers, sisters, husbands and partners can lift up and support women.

There needs to be a conversation about the role of partners in the road to recovery, not only about their role in a supportive manner but also the impact it has on someone when their wife or partner is experiencing such extreme mental health issues. Partners need support too.

I have through this experience reached such a positive point in my life, where I am giving back to the mental health team what they gave to me. I will be a lifelong supporter of these services.

Now, every time I hold my daughter close and she smiles up at me, there is no self-doubt, there is no fear. I know she is smiling because she is with her mama, she is where she first started, where she came into being.

When I blow raspberries on her tummy and she screams in delight, when I make silly faces and she copies me, when she clambers on me to squeeze me close and breathe in my scent, I am present in all of these moments. I know they are for me, and I feel so blessed and so very lucky to be her mother.

The feelings of not being enough aren't there any more. I know I am enough. I know she loves me. I am her mother and she is my child. I think about how I was afraid to kiss her when she was so small and it seems so alien to me.

I am so blessed to be in the space that I am in now, that I can stand tall and say PND did not get the best of me.

The best of me belongs to my daughter and my husband. Post-natal depression doesn't mean that you will be lost forever.

The bravest thing you can do when you are suffering like

I did, is to reach out to your GP or midwife. Take the first step and you will be shown a path that leads back to you.

I sometimes think about those moments lost, the black fog that hung over me and crippled me, but I mourn the loss of that time less and less with each passing day.

The moments I enjoy now, the intense love I feel, the oneness and the closeness I feel with my daughter is the greatest gift and blessing which I appreciate every single day.

AFSHAN HUSSAIN

Afshan Hussain is an experienced, outstanding educator

with a background in teaching Science.

She has teaching experience across West Yorkshire as well as the West Midlands where she served as lead Science teacher before rapidly progressing to the role of head of the Science faculty in an inner-city Birmingham Secondary School. In this role she was described as an "outstanding practitioner" and highly praised by the Deputy Regional Schools Commissioner at the Department for Education (DfE).

Afshan's creative flair has also led her to work within the beauty industry as a fully qualified and trained hair and make-up artist as well as being a self-taught intricate henna artist.

Since taking a career break to focus on spending time with her daughter and raising a family, Afshan has used her knowledge and experience as an educator as well as her personal journey to raise awareness within the South Asian community about key mental health issues such as eating disorders and post-natal depression.

Afshan has worked alongside women's mental health teams on a voluntary basis to offer insight into services and to help adapt programmes that will be used to engage mothers with mental health concerns.

Afshan is keen to encourage and empower women to seek

help and not to allow perceived cultural boundaries to hold them back from recovery.

Afshan's mantra is to 'Be the change you want to see in society" and so she hopes to shine a light on this taboo subject by referring to her personal struggles and journey to recovery.

Her mission is to give hope and support to women who are suffering and to pass on the knowledge that positive outcomes can be reached with the correct help and support.

Her desire is to cultivate an environment where members of the South Asian community are knowledgeable and pro-active about addressing maternal mental health issues.

Contact:

Email:

my_pnd_journey@outlook.com

Facebook:

(Group) PND Support in the Asian Community: https://www.facebook.com/groups/446692336188571/

 instagram.com/lilly_and_mama

4

NEVER GIVE UP HOPE IN LIFE… THERE IS ALWAYS A HAPPY ENDING TO LOOK FORWARD TOO…

y journey of life has been an unpredictable rollercoaster of many ups and downs, which we all go through in life. But when I now look back at the past, I smile, as it has made me who I am today, a strong, independent and successful woman.

I am happy because I made decisions throughout my life experience that at that time seemed so difficult, but they were well worth it in the end.

Being the youngest daughter of a Muslim family, you could say I was very spoilt, and was always loved so much by everyone. I have been very overprotected, and always got what I wanted. I know I had the best childhood ever and I am very thankful to my parents.

I studied very hard through my time at George Dixon

International School & Sixth Form Centre, but then there was a turn just after Year Nine. This is when I got mixed in the wrong crowd. My grades started slipping. The sooner I realised, the better it would be for me.

Being in this particular wrong crowd meant I had less time concentrating on my studies and more time just chilling. To be honest, I was losing focus on the main priorities and when my Head Teacher, Sir Robert Dowling, sat me down and told me, "Don't let anyone affect the grades you are capable of," it was a turning point for me to fix my priorities and to get things sorted before it was too late.

This was when I realised that these people who are meant to be your friends at these important stages of your studies in life, are in fact the biggest influences at this age. As this is where you can get distracted so easily, to get dragged down, to under achieve in your real abilities of success.

It was in Year Eleven when I realised my GCSEs were at stake and believe me, I wanted to get my 7 A-Cs and I knew I had to just back off from the crowd and focus on what was important to me at that precise moment. I just put my mind to it, and I worked extremely hard.

At a young age I attended Children's University at St

Patrick's Catholic School Church, and since then I always had the vision that one day I would go to university and get my degree.

So having that focus in my mind I just had to make sure others, including my own friends, did not influence me and did not distract me and I just focused on myself. Sometimes you just have to do what is best for you, for your own best interest. The end result will be a happy ending because you know you worked hard for it.

After putting time, effort and hard work in, I passed my GCSEs with flying colours. I still remember the day of my results like it was yesterday. I was literally jumping for joy the whole way home from school, and my parents were so proud.

Their smiles meant the world to me. In life, what you achieve for yourself makes you feel proud and that's what makes your parents proud as they would always want what's best for you.

So even when you have the little doubt in your head that you feel you can't do it or you think you're going to fail, just take some deep breaths, have a little break and make little action points to get yourself ready to aim at where you want to really be and reach your goal.

School wasn't always very easy. I did get bullied for

being very skinny, but I was a bright student and had good friends too. I always tried to focus on passing my studies and I had to make myself strong.

I did not let the bullies get to me. I just started by ignoring them. You see, silence is a big key in life, as bullies want you to react to them and when they know you are not bothered they will just leave you alone eventually.

I used to get called names about myself, being so skinny but I was happy in a way because basically, I thought to myself, I could eat so much food and never put weight on, so it was great. And I still do love my food, burgers, chips, pizza and pasta.

You just have to enjoy life. Once you're happy within yourself your confidence reaches the skies and you can be whoever you want to be. So I always turned the negativity into something positive and my mind was set free.

After my GCSEs, I did my A levels in Business & I.C.T and yet again, I got distracted like you do sometimes, and would leave my coursework to just a few weeks before my deadlines but I didn't give up. Life will throw you so much from all angles, but you have to face things, get them organised and just get it done.

These distractions happened because I started working at the young age of sixteen at Woolworths & Lloyds Pharmacy. These two jobs were great whilst I was doing my A levels but then Asda opened in Cape Hill and YES, I got myself a third job. I just enjoy communicating with others by giving any help or support I can provide to them. Tackling three part time jobs and studying for my A-levels was hard work but I really enjoyed it.

Working from a young age I felt more independent in myself, financially, you know – not always asking parents for money or relying on anyone else.

I was in my own world, gaining satisfaction and becoming more popular, networking more with others and from a young age I always had a passion for talking to people, getting to know them. I still know people from back then that are now my good friends. You see, in life people will always come and go in your life journey of success.

But you will know yourself what is best for you and which people will be there for you to help and support you, but no one can ever stop you from getting to your goal. At the end of the day it is all dependent on your own actions and motivation to achieve your dream.

I was doing extremely well. I was leader in all my retail

jobs; in Asda I was running my own Deli Department. Life was great. Life is never easy as you know, and tackling my three jobs and studies was my choice and yet again, using my experience at GCSE level, I got motivated, made an action plan, a list and a timetable that suited me. I created my own deadlines and worked hard and I passed my A levels.

It just shows, the more effort you put into something the more successful you will be. This was an incredible achievement for me, because I never gave up hope in life.

I always think that if you have got a goal in life, you have to overcome the barriers and obstacles. You just need to get what you want by tackling the distractions and focus on your vision.

Your vision is your desire and your aim, and once you take a step towards it this is when your journey begins. Don't ever think you can't do it; yes, we all have those down days and think, "I can't do it, I just can't do it," and sometimes we are stressed about one hundred and one things, as we have so much on our minds, but you have to make yourself get up, and be strong and take even a little step towards making your dream a reality.

I had achieved my A levels and I was looking forward to going to University soon, and then I had a misfortune. I had to give up my one of my jobs (to begin with), and this was all based on jealousy from others, including work colleagues, and I was getting poorly from doing too much at once.

You see, in life certain people around you will always be in competition with you. There are so many characters, personalities that you will come across, but it will be your choice whom you trust. Not everyone is what they seem, but that's part of life, and this is when you realise who is your real friend and who isn't.

Working in retail was never easy, especially being successful at young age, everyone asking, "Why have you got three jobs?" etc. It was my choice to have three jobs and it definitely kept me busy for sure, but the main thing was I enjoyed it and I didn't care less what others thought of me. I have always believed that at the end of the day, no one is putting food on my table except me. No one else is paying my bills. The fact is you do all this for yourself so why live up to others' expectations and influences if it's not worth your happiness> Be you and be yourself.

In life I have lost good friends, even people I grew up with that I had known since I was in nappies. This was because of people interfering, including my own family and relatives but I feel as you get older you realise it doesn't matter about the number of people in your circle. It is all about the quality of people you choose to have in your circle.

So, I gave up one job where I was a manager and I became the talk of the town because rumours were being spread about me... "What happened? Why did you leave? Was it too much for you?" … etc.

I was actually getting ready to focus on going to University. You see, people will always, especially in some Asian communities, assume things and judge you for all sorts, from what you're wearing, what you're doing, always questioning why this and that, but I always have and always will stand up for myself.

I used to answer the haters back and say it straight: "First look what is going on in your household before judging me." I didn't really care what people thought of me because they don't control me. Only you can control yourself and make those paths for yourself and trust yourself to aim for your success. Only Allah can judge me. This is my belief till the day I die.

Society's backward way of thinking is an issue. I can see it is being tackled in the 21st century, but it has always been a problem. You shouldn't let anyone one tell you that you're not good enough, or this is how it should be, or this is how you should do this.

Don't ever let anyone control you or your emotions. Yes, it is hard to say no to some people and to make choices, but sometimes you have to say No because it's the best thing to do.

Never let anyone undermine you. You don't need drama in your life for no reason. Over my years and experiences, I have let go of friends and even relatives because of the drama that was associated with them.

You see, I have always been straight up, and don't believe in telling stories behind people's backs. I have always said it to their face and exactly how it is.

Being honest is the best policy and you will have no regret within yourself. I basically just say how it is. Don't ever let people who live near you, especially in your community, judge you. Let them talk about you. Show them it doesn't bother you. They will always move on to another story and it will just continue with someone else.

The main principle is that you are true to yourself. A long as you know you are right and not doing wrong to anyone, don't care about others who want you to feel down.Ignore people like that and concentrate on you, yourself and your future. Your life is your choices. I made decisions because I had to for myself and my misfortunes turned in to fortunes.

So, I had some unfortunate experiences, some very unlucky experiences. I became very ill over an eleven month period, and I decided to quit and resigned my other two jobs. This was an eye-opening experience.

From working three jobs on the ladder to success, I became ill all of sudden and this was a major change for me. So, from being a workaholic I was at a standstill in life.

I stopped my work commitments, my studies, and didn't go University straight away. My illness was devastating. I wasn't myself, but I did push myself to get better thanks to my brilliant Doctor P. Madhavan, and Nurse Yvonne from Cavendish Medical Practice.

Reality hit me hard. There were no friends or relatives that were really there for me. If they were it was just for gossip related reasons. I had my immediate family's support including my grandparents and aunties.

But that was it. My friends turned their backs on me, even the ones I worked with for years. They just vanished into thin air. At that point in time I felt I was nonexistent; I was nothing. I wasn't important to anyone, you know.

There were no feelings or consideration from people I thought were my friends.

I felt as if everyone had turned against me. But you know what? I didn't give up hope; I turned the negative vibes into positive ones. I just had to. I had no choice because I had to recover for myself and for my family.

I had great willpower, with help and support from my family, especially my elder sister, Tahria Bibi who was my inspiration and still is. My sister is the eldest in the family. She is a successful primary school teacher. She was my mentor.

She has always given me the best advice amongst my family. This is when I realised who is there for you when you need them the most.

My family helped turn my dark days to a bright future, by helping me regain my health and getting me back on my own two feet.

Whilst I was poorly I remember my dad, Mr Mahmood Khan, who was not far from being retired, travelling long distances for work. In his last few weeks, working for the Corus Company, my dad made a decision and took an early retirement for me. I will never forget that sacrifice my dad made for me. He held me one day and was trying to make me drink my meal replacements soups. I was very weak, and I would only drink from my father's hand. My parents' prayers were for me to get better and well. He fed me that soup and told me he would be home a lot more just for me, so I could get better and back on my feet.

He said, "I just want my daughter back, who was always on her feet running around job to job, studying, smiling, bubbly and just happy." My dad retired early and looked after me and my family. And he still does, bless him, and mum was happy to see me recovering well.

My dad, Mr Mahmood Khan, has worked his entire life, providing for us as a family and I am so thankful for that. I even went to the same secondary school as my dad, which was great. Now he's retired he works for the local Dudley Road Mosque and enjoys life.

My parents spend six months here and six months abroad in Pakistan. That's a lifestyle they have chosen, and it suits them well. Over the years, we as family have adapted very well to it.

Sometimes in life you have to make sacrifices to help others and it's the best feeling ever. I do miss my parents when they go abroad, but they need their break just as I like to have a break too, so you have more understanding of other people's feelings and viewpoints.

Changes are not always easy, especially when your routine changes drastically. I went from having three jobs to none. It was a massive change for my system but I just had to do what I had to do at the time and it was the best decision I could have made.

I learned to adapt to a new environment. It isn't always easy, but it becomes easier the more you work well in that environment. I mean, I worked in massive food retail companies like Asda and Morrisons and you just have to put time, effort and have the main focus on board. That is, have courage, will power, and the confidence to do what makes you fit in any situation comfortably.

You have to lose some things to gain much more in life. You will be much happier in life just for being appreciated, and recognised for your helpful thoughts and considerations. I never thought I would become so ill but I did and I didn't give up hope. I fought hard, focused and kept my vision in my head, and just dreamt of that graduation gown and the cap on my head. I just wanted to see my whole family so proud of me.

My parents, my grandparents, my brothers, Shazad, Ikhtiaz and Hasrat, my sister, Tahria, and my aunties Tehzeem and Saleem, all helped me so much on my road to recovery and I wouldn't have been able to overcome this obstacle in my life without their help and support.

After eleven months of illness, I was fully recovered and well and back on my feet and feeling more myself.

When I was well again the decision was made for me to go on a holiday, and I flew to Pakistan with my Mum. I stayed for three months and I had a good break and then I came back fresh, to start my new life all over again.

You see, if you have a setback in life, it doesn't mean it's the end of the world. You need to put these extenuating circumstances into place to focus it into positive actions.

Feel free and think to yourself: my life is not going the way I planned it, but I am alive, breathing and there is still purpose on this earth for my existence. That's when you start planning, even if it is the smallest action plan, it has to begin with something to get that happy ending you've always desired.

Parents always want what's best for their children. Even if you think if they are too strict or controlling sometimes, they do it out of love for you to become successful because they want you to be happy.My family has always been a great support even when I would sometimes think something else. In the long run they always had my best interests at heart even though it might not have felt that way at the time.

I was home from Pakistan, back on my feet and I got a

job at TK Maxx, in the Bullring in my hometown of Birmingham. However, it wasn't long before I had to quit once again, and my routine changed because of unfortunate situations.

During this time, I lost my granddad and I couldn't face going back to work. When you lose someone so close to you, your life does change but you have to just imagine and wish they are watching over you and they want what's best for you too.

My granddad was a loving man, a popular man in our neighborhood community, Mr Mohd Khan. He was always helping others, being there for everyone, so kindhearted and just full of happiness.

Bereavements are never easy. They affect your emotions and make you feel overwhelmed and full of mixed emotions, but you have to focus for your good mindset and get yourself together and focus on your own life because no one else will.

I had a short break from work and then went back working for Avon, then Arcedia Direct as the Marketing Sales Team Manager.

Things were looking good; I was back to my old ways because I kept trying. I was always taught that if one job goes another will follow. I then started working for Helen

E at Debenhams, which I enjoyed, and had a great opportunity to work at The Clothes Show event at the NEC.

I just enjoyed working with people so much. I had quite a few career changes. I went to work for Hisbah Accountants as an Assistant Clerk and I gained so many skills and experiences. From there I did some administration work at the Aston Arena.

Then I felt I was well enough. I felt I was ready to focus and concentrate on my studies. I finally got myself a place at Staffordshire University, studying Business Management.

I was so thrilled when I got my place at University. It was the most precious feeling and it felt so wonderful that my journey had begun, and I was going to reach my goal.

I started my studies in a new town, in Stoke-on-Trent. I made new friends and started my career in Business Management Studies at a degree level. I started my degree in 2009. Oh, yes, it was another rollercoaster to achieve my degree, but I got there in the end.

I had so many ups and downs, but from past experiences I had the mindset that I would never give up in life, not ever. And I kept going and going till I knew I would get that gown on and wear that hat on my head and get that degree.

I started my course as a full time degree, then, due to more unfortunate circumstances I went part time, and then took a break from studies altogether and got a job as a Dental Nurse at Lozell's Dental Surgery. After only a few weeks in this role, I got my myself the job I'd always wanted, as a supervisor in Morrisons.

It was brilliant. I started working at Edgbaston Morrisons in Five Ways full time and was running and managing the Deli department. I truly enjoyed it, with great support from the other managers, Pete, Sikander, Mike, Dan and Sue. Retail work in the food industry took a lot of time, effort, and commitment and it was fun.

But yet again I faced people that would do anything to make you not succeed. This was just people and I thought to myself, you know what? Ignore the haters and just do what I am best at, which was leading people.

The team of managers became my family at work, expectations were raised and it was a successful road.

My dream and my ambition came into my mind, and my life's goal was to get my degree. I felt bad at that time that I had left it incomplete, but I was always turning the negativity to positivity.

I was gaining my managerial experience so that was the positive outcome of working full time and studying part time instead. Whilst working at Morrisons full time, I found it hard, struggling with a thirty-nine hours plus contract whilst continuing my studies. So, I made the decision and left my job and went back to my studies full time. It was actually a hard decision, but it was the best decision I've ever made in my life.

In life, some decisions you just have to make. It is probably not what you want to decide at the time but in the long run it is actually the best option for your own future and to allow you to achieve your overall goals.

So I went back to University and I got motivated and put my mind to my studies. I fought all odds and barriers by putting all my personal issues and problems aside to get my degree.

I worked extremely hard to get my studies completed.

During my studies I did get a part time job at Kidderminster Pharmacy, through an old connection from working at Lloyds Pharmacy.

A manager remembered me from back then when he was a P-Reg Pharmacist. He was now the successful owner of his own pharmacy and offered me a part time job.

I was grateful to my boss, Am, who gave me a job working at his pharmacy, as this helped me with my studies, as well as financially. I worked in the retail sector of the pharmacy and this was effective in enhancing my knowledge and skills in business management.

Yet again, third time around after doing my GCSEs and A levels, my deadlines came and this time it was the real deal: it was for my undergraduate degree.

I did it again. I didn't lose hope or focus, and I formed an action plan, put deadlines in place, and I smashed it. I was able to change my overall grade within a few weeks. That's how determined and motivated I was because I knew deep down I could achieve my degree at the level I wanted and I did it.

It just goes to show that if you really want something, I mean really, from the bottom of your heart, you want to do something, then you can achieve it, and nobody – and I mean no one in the world – can stop you getting what you want.

In life you have to communicate to your own thoughts first, then fight the negativity and overcome it and beat it with success and the only way to do this is with positive thinking.

You can't imagine the negative energy I went through

that brought me down so hard that it made me want to give up. But I walked away from that bad area where nobody deserves to be.

It has always helped me to write things down. I now have a passion planner diary and it is one of the best diaries I have ever had. It helps you to concentrate on your life journey, your goals, and is so useful. Furthermore, I worked yet again extremely hard and I made sure I got my gown and hat on, and I did it.

I graduated and it was one of the best days of my life. I finally did it and graduated successfully. My parents and family came to my graduation and it was the proudest moment for my parents. To see them smile and their tears of joy was an incredible journey.

I am ever so thankful to everyone who supported me, especially Angela Lawrence, my tutor at University. Also Vicky Roberts, Paul Dobson and Sue Fisher, Judith my mentor, Lesley Mountford, Elsa Heffernan and Lisa Benson my student support team. Especially Neil Morrison and Amanda Packham who gave me the opportunity in 2014 to complete my degree when I thought I would never have a chance to.

This was because I just was going through so much during that time and I needed that support help from the

Staffordshire University staff. I completed my degree finally in 2016.

It was the biggest achievement of my life. This was it. I now had in life what I had dreamed of achieving – my goal, by getting my Business Management Degree. So, no matter what you go through in life always strive to gain your goal. You have to own it with pride and chase your dreams for success.

I finally accomplished my dream and to get there I had the support of these people and I will cherish them for life, especially the staff at Staffordshire University, who were so helpful, thoughtful and were always there for me when I needed someone.

There were moments I wanted to give up on everything because I had so much going on and at moments I did become lost, but I overcame the negativity. I did this by reminding myself where it was I wanted to be, and what I wanted to achieve.

It was a hard, rocky road but I finally saw the bright light at the end of the tunnel, glistening. Memories that you cherish in life are what make you happy and looking forward within yourself to be the person you want to be, is the best feeling ever. So, don't ever think for a slightest second you can't do something because you can if you put your mind to it and focus on it.

In life I have met good and bad people, had many experiences but you have to remember never hold grudges because I never did. Just let them be. If they want to reach out to you, let them. Otherwise you can do it yourself and on your own you can achieve anything in the world.

Throughout my life and studying experiences I did suffer from anxiety, trying to do too much at once. It can be stressful but it's the way I learned coping strategies and methods to manage everything. I had to put my principles in order to focus more on gaining what I needed, and to do that was indeed the most important part of it all.

Time management is such a crucial element in life, whatever stage of life you are going through. If you plan things right, in order and in advance, everything will work well, with structures in place that feel right for the result to be what you need it to be.

Sometimes in life. even in your worst days and during those darkest moments in life, you will never ever forget those people that helped you the most throughout your hardships. You have to appreciate those that are good to

you as you never know one day they may need you. I
have got close friends that I would cherish for life;

Uncle Khalid, Amanda, Mohammed, Hanna, Sonia,
Nazmeen, Alisha, Nusrat, Nilofer, Razia... and there are
too many to name, but they know who they are. Even
people I worked with like Am, Raman, Han, Tony,
Sohail, Adnan, Qasim, Toqir, Jodie, Naheem, Sundeep.

My entire family including my parents and siblings,
grandparents, aunties, uncles and my lovely nieces,
Saleha, Samihah, Madiyah, Ummayyah, Malaika, Eliza,
my nephews Raiyan and Zeeshan , my family and cousins
Baji Naheed & Rizwana, Muzreen, Zeenat and Afsana
and the list goes on and on, but people know deep down
they are appreciated for helping and supporting me
always.

My brother Ikhtiaz (known as Iky) has also been my
biggest support and has always been there for me no
matter what. He always has and still does help me with
reaching out to positive goals. He is also my inspiration
and has a heart of gold, so caring and loving for others
always. Without his help and support and that of his wife
Baji Naheed, I would not be where I am today. Baji
Naheed did everything for me when I was single and
even now when I am married, always giving me so much

love and treating me like her own sister and I love my whole family for that.

Hasrat supported me also in so many ways. He loves doing everyone's job and helping out with whatever he can and that is amazing. Shazad is great too and as an elder brother has always been very supportive.

My parents have always been there for me and are so loving and caring and always gave me whatever I wanted and I love them so much for everything. My life would not be the same without all my close family and friends around.

Sometimes the thing that will make a big difference in your life is just having someone listening to you and talking to you about anything you want to share with them. Anything can help if you give it a try. Without the support from friends and family and work colleagues it wouldn't have been easy to cope with everything. At some stages in my life, even with help – it was hard, but I pulled through and became a winner.

Even if you're all on your own and you're starting from scratch, yes it is a big step, but you just have to get on with it and get it all done. Once it is accomplished then you will ultimately feel amazing, proud and most importantly you will feel yourself.

I got my degree and I continued working for Kidderminster Pharmacy. Joys of work, helping four pharmacies shape up their retail shops was something I enjoyed. Managing the merchandising and project managing the stores was giving me plenty of experience.

Everything was going fine. I had the opportunity after my degree to start my Masters in HR and I just went for it. I started it whilst I was working at the pharmacy. It was good. After almost completing a year I had to make a life changing decision, whether to continue with my studies or get married to the love of my life.

Decisions, decisions, decisions: they are so important in life and one decision you make can change the whole future for you automatically.But only you, yourself can decide what you what to do and decide and reflect on it, to do what is best for yourself and not for anyone else. Only you as a person can control what your future holds for you. I made the decision and I got married to my best friend, the love of my life, Mr Taz Ali.I took a break from studies after deciding to get married. I was enjoying the wonders of married life and I got my happy ever after. I am now a happily married housewife living with my in-laws, just the four of us and it's amazing. I have everything I ever wanted and could ever dream of.

Now I feel so much closer to my overall life goal. I

gained my success in life through studies and work, gained my happiness in life and love and successfully settled with my own family life, and life just goes on and on. It never stops for anyone.

Time doesn't stop; always remember the clock is always ticking, every minute of the day. Changes from minute to minutes, hour to hours, day to days, week to weeks, into a month, then months into a year and then it is going by in years. Time will continue so you need to stop wasting time thinking, "What if?"

The negativity needs to go out of the window. Stop thinking, "What if this happened?" and "What if that happened?" You need to stop right there, put a line through it and start afresh because it's never too late to make changes for the prospect of your better future.

I couldn't wait to get married to Mr Taz Ali; he is so special to me. In the Asian communities it is traditional tohave a big lavish wedding, but I didn't want that. I had a lovely small ceremony at Zauq's Buffet at Star City and had fewer than fifty guests, just my immediate family and a few friends, and it was beautiful.

It was a dream wedding. I couldn't imagine anything better and when I look back over the years and everything I went through I would never have imagined that I would be where I am today, living in the countryside with the love of my life and blessed with a lovely family.

I moved away from my home town of Birmingham. Of course, this wasn't an easy decision, but it was the best choice I've ever made. Moving forward in life is not always how you plan it to be: moving homes, moving areas, moving jobs, meeting new people. It is all part of life.

You have to take it one day at a time, and realise that if you work hard and you are good at what you do you can do anything in life. Never give up hope.

Motivation is always the key for anything and anyone to be successful. Whether it is for yourself, your business, or whatever it is, you need to focus, put your positive energy in it and realise your true potential.

So I have had a break from work and studies for a while, enjoying my married life and soon one day I know my aim is to complete my Master's Degree and I will because I am determined to.

So, I am going to go back to my studies and back to work and plan start my own family one day. I know from my life journey, if you didn't get what you wanted at one moment of time in life, you definitely will at some stage.

You can always put some plans on hold if you need to, and if your circumstances change for a while, never live in regret as you can go back to it and start again, at the next opportunity that arises for your success.

I have made great relationships with people over my life journey and lost close people too. I lost both my granddads years ago and one of my grandmas passed away last year.

At the time of a bereavement it is extremely hard to accept that people whom you have loved have all of sudden left the world, but their memories will be cherished forever.

Losing someone is hard. It was very painful for me but life moves on, and yes, you still have to get up and get ready and do your day to day duties in whatever you do in life, and do what you can for people. For those that have left you, all you can do is just pray for them.

I have always helped people whenever they've needed my help; the important thing for me is that I was doing something good for someone no matter what. Some people will take advantage of you, as others will appreciate you. It's all part of the journey of life.

People pass away; people are born: it's life. It is a healing process in the concepts of life, and it is so important to not let anyone get in the way of you becoming who you want to be. Set your goal and achieve it.

Trust is a major impact in everyone's life. For me, trust and honesty are so important. It is important because once you lose trust in someone it is so hard to get it back. Forgive and forget is not so simple.

So yes, life throws barriers. You need to face them in the best possible way, to interact with your inner emotions and gain that power to be confident. I have had experiences where I have been betrayed, lied to by people I know. As I got older, I learned to forgive but found it hard to forget.

But then slowly you just let it go because in life as you're aiming for your dream goal, these triumphs just become a blare in the background, and you start to concentrate on what is more important in life, in empowering your goals.

Some people I forgave for things that hurt me at that time. We are all human beings and we do make mistakes and learn to make things right.

I learned the best way forward is to forgive and move on. People have broken my trust in the past and it hurts because in life you don't expect it from the close circle of people around you, but then I realised they wanted to earn it back and that was my choice and now things are good with those people.

You never know what is around the corner. What is going to happen tomorrow? I don't even know if I will wake up tomorrow and be alive. So, yes I am thankful every day, for everything I have and for everyone who is in my life – I feel so blessed. You just have to have faith in yourself and think, "I can do this" and figure out a way in which you are going to get there.

I went through a period of time when I was alone, but I got out there and researched how I was going to get to the end goal. I am successful now, because I am who I am, and I wouldn't change myself for anyone.

After everything that I have been through, I can't imagine not being where I am today. It's because of all the difficulties I went through, changes in all angles and aspects of life, meeting different people, networking, communicating with others.This is how I have learned. By talking to others it helped me so much in the past. It's the sense of relief you get just by talking about all your feelings to anyone, and getting it off your chest. It makes you think about your life and makes you realise what's best for you.

Sometimes talking to other people helps. For some it

could be talking to health professionals like counsellors, or you could talk aloud or just keep a diary.

Everyone is different and have their own coping strategies that suits them best. So, find your best methods of coping and use it to fight the barriers that prevent you from being your best self.

Your feelings are always in your own control. To help, you can share them with anyone but remember that is your personal choice. Throughout my life I have gained a lot of valuable experiences throughout the highs and lows, but I got there in the end and got my happy ending but still want to achieve more in life and nothing will stop me achieving my goals in life.

I have always been ambitious from a very young age, in my work careers, especially in retail management, but I worked hard for it. When I worked at Asda I got the job first just as a normal worker and during my training period I was selected as a Team Leader and was running my own department because my Manager noticed my enhanced abilities of leading a team.

It wasn't easy as I was the youngest in the team and I had to delegate tasks to members of staff that were older than me. I was only seventeen at that time. But wherever you go in the world, people will notice the hard work you put in, and value your attributes and qualities and this will indeed boost not only your confidence but enhance your career options too and you will build better relationships overall.

Then years later I worked for Morrisons and then a Pharmacy. Now being a housewife it's still working with people. It made me realise how much our mothers actually do for us, whilst we are being busy with our own lives.

Whatever I have done it's my actions that have made me who I am, and I can't tell you the feeling from the moment you achieve even one of your dreams in life to your overall goal in life. It is something which is better than anything.

Breaks: we need them, oh yes, we do for sure. I mean, we all deserve a break, a day just in our pjs, or a day out, a few days out, a weekend away, or even a week or weeks, months away or just some time for yourself. My favourite "time out' is shopping even though I have calmed down a lot now.

We all need to give our brains a rest and a good time out. I always felt the best method of relaxation is to have any sort of break you desire; anything that make you happy.

After a break, I have always felt refreshed and ready to go again with life.

A break away does you good and treating yourself never hurts. I also love having full body massages and facials because that's what helps me feel better and relaxed. We all as individuals will always have different coping methods for different situations, so don't be afraid to try something different. It may work for you, it may not, but don't be scared to try something new.

You'll never know till it's been tested, and it may be beneficial for you. Holidays are great, even if it's a break in the country. A change of scenery might help you relax and make you feel better. Being in a different environment can make a difference. Choose what is best for you, and when it is best for you. Never feel that you're on your own, have faith in your God, and you will be fine.

My religion is really important. Being a Muslim is what I was born into and it is who I am and I am thankful forAllah, for everything I have been through and for everything I have now. I am so grateful that I have amazing parents, and family, and I have my happy ever after with my husband.

I am thankful to my parents and to all my family and

friends for always being there for me in life and I appreciate them for just being who they are and always will.

The wait for true love was well worth it and I love my husband dearly. He is my everything. He isn't just my partner, he is my best friend, and I know that he is somebody who will always be there for me. Mr Taz Ali, thank-you so much for everything. Just being with my husband and knowing he is so understanding and caring,

I do feel like I am really lucky to be his wife and may Allah bless us with many more years to come. Ameen. In Shaa Allah. I feel blessed with having so many lovely people in my life and I will never forget where I came from.

Where you come from is what you are, and it is your identity. I have been through a lot in life, but I never gave up and that is the main reason for my success now.

One step forward will get you to walk one mile, and thenfrom that one mile your journey will begin and will start to grow to become more successful than you could ever imagine.

Only you, yourself, can turn your negative energy to high levels of positive energy. In this world all you have to do is never give up and just keep going. It may take days, weeks, months, a year or even years to accomplish your dream goal, as we all have different life situations, different life styles and commitments, but you can make it work just by taking that one step to your goal – to be successful.

You will get your happy ending one day just like I did, and now I am so happy in life and still have so much to achieve because you should never lose hope. Always dream and reach out for your goals.

Even those dark days will become bright and you just need to take action, have the motivation and dedication to become the empowering person that you deserve to be.

There is always light at the end of tunnels. Positive thinking is the way forward, and never give up hope in life… there is always a happy ending to look forward to.

AISHA SAMERA KHAN

Aisha Khan is a hard working individual who knows her values.

She is aware of what she desires in life and knows exactly how to take responsibility for herself and her actions.

She is a highly experienced sales person, with over thirteen years of experience and has gained excellent knowledge in both the retail and the pharmaceutical industry.

She has achieved management leadership along with positive desires to succeed in life and is motivated in learning new skills frequently.

Aisha has great experience in retail fashion and in the food industries.

Aisha has worked with her own energy and resources to build a network throughout her work experiences, including social media links via LinkedIn, Facebook, Snapchat and Instagram, building international recognition in helping and talking to others regarding their issues and problems and has resonated with a wide global audience.

Aisha is a great listener and loves to help others with advice, guidance and support all the way to their goals of success.

Aisha has always focused on development and opportunities to enhance her prospects for herself and for others.

She enjoys public relations and community partnerships and helping anyone to gain and overcome obstacles and difficulties in a better way.

Aisha has a proven record of success in interacting and communicating with others from diverse ethno-cultural and racial backgrounds.

Aisha is always devoted to others at any time.

Aisha is very energetic with high levels of extensive customer service skills, with the ability to resolve issues effectively with superb interpersonal skills.

Aisha has achieved a great network through excellent verbal and written communications.

Aisha speaks fluently in English, Urdu, Mirpuri and Punjabi languages and is an effective Team leader.

She has achieved so much in life, by balancing three jobs whilst studying and achieved her goals through dedication and motivation.

Aisha is optimistic and has also worked for charities including Muslim Aid and British Heart Foundation by raising donations and organising events.

Aisha has worked closely with others in setting up events for the local communities and places of worship including Mosques and Churches.

Aisha has gained many awards and achievements in her life.

She gained a 2:1 Degree in Business Management.

She achieved her City & Guilds Retail Certificate as well as completing a Computer Based Learning training in Health and Safety and Food Hygiene.

She has worked at the N.E.C. Clothes show and was one of the top sellers for Helen-E Cosmetics.

Aisha's Mission is to help others gain their confidence and to never give up hope in life with their dreams and loves to share her own personal experiences to help others overcome barriers for them to be successful.

Aisha has had several successful roles and can mentor others to power up and become more enthusiastic, confident, and ambitious and gain skills with the ability to work independently as well as in a team.

Aisha feels when individuals go through different levels of experiences, including severe life stressors and trauma, it isn't easy for anyone for their lives to unravel.

Her passion is to help others with better communications so they are able to strengthen their inner motivation skills and deal with emotions in a better way. So, they can feel themselves that they are aiming and reaching out to their goals successfully.

Aisha Khan reflects her commitments in provision of

excellence in customer service in Retail and Human Resources management and to better client's prospects in life.

Contact:

Email:

aisha.samera.khan@gmail.com

Linkedin: Aisha Samera Khan

Facebook: Aisha Samera Khan

instagram.com/aisha.samera.khan786

snapchat.com/add/aishaskhan786

5

WAS A WOMAN CREATED TO BE A PUPPET?

"Y̲ou don't need to work. Look after your home." "You're a Mum: your home is your priority."

"What will people say when they hear you go to events or travel?"

"Anxiety? Depression? Nothing is wrong with you. Stop exaggerating."

"Take care of everyone else: thats your life goal."

Was a woman created to be a Puppet? Of course not. Does she have more to life than creating babies and looking after her forever home? YES!

A mixture of culture and society has ruined the purpose of a Woman in the 21st Century. Let me tell you, you were created with a purpose and don't let any culture or society take that away from you. Before I reveal my identity, let me remind you of yours …

You are half the society and you raise the other half!

This is the story of how a suicidal, severely depressed and unstable woman/mum/wife went from being admitted to hospital forty three times, and nearly divorced, to a nourished relationship, moved homes and created a storm in her new company within seven weeks!

Hi, my name is Ashii Akram and this is my my story…

One daughter of two, our parents raised us like princesses. Coming from a Kashmiri background, we saw many boundaries which limited what we could and couldn't do, down to barriers created by our culture and society.

But we weren't going to stop. We started working in my father's hard built business from the age of seven. YES, SEVEN!

We learned the value of work and money from a young age when he would have me and my sister (who has more of a business head than me – lol) making boxes competitively for a couple of pounds and we loved the adrenaline and competition every time.

I was the typical daughter. I loved business studies so pursued it through education and graduated but then did nothing with it and was working in retail.

The life changing chapter in any woman's life, Marriage. Boy, was it life changing! I married my best friend and my soul mate. Two years of fighting an arranged proposal to have a love marriage was bloody hard, but alhamdulillah I got there in the end! But little did I know how my life would change so much...

With marriage comes compromise, sacrifices and a lifetime of changes. My biggest struggle was giving up the princess crown I had worn from the day I was born, not because I'm awkward but because I was assuming everyone would treat me the way my parents always treated me, no matter where I was, but of course that's not always the case. Patience is virtue, as they say.

My first born arrived instantly as I fell pregnant straight away after getting married and along with him came postnatal depression. Living with in laws at the time I was petrified of being judged for my mental health so I always found myself brushing it under the carpet, but this only caused one thing: shit hitting the fan (excuse my language)!

My son was only 3 months, and MAT pay wasn't doing

anything so I joined on of those "work from home" companies and let me tell you: BEST DECISION EVER! I didn't earn anything for it to change my circumstances at the time, I'll be honest.

But it helped me change and gave me a divert of attention as I was around women just like me, women that were mentally and physically drained and needed guidance.

You see, the problem with our society and culture is that people would rather see you struggling and at rock bottom instead of thriving and succeeding.

There is more to a woman than her marriage, her house, her mental health and her children but our society constantly limits us. Why?

I found that the deeper you look into homes the more similar patterns you see for the women, like birds trapped in a cage.

My marriage wasn't working out at the time. There were faults at both ends with a mixture of interference. And it was even harder to digest my reality as it was my own choice, a love marriage. After forty eight admissions to hospital, many suicide attempts, a broken marriage and a completely shattered woman, things were about to change! DEAL WITH IT is what we are taught as women, SHHH AND JUST GET ON WITH IT!

But that only results in one thing: death. I couldn't deal with my reality, my relationships, motherhood and poor finances which resulted in an overdose when I was in hospital. Do you know who gave a shit? Nobody! No, I'm being serious. Nobody.

You know who picked me up from rock bottom and said, enough is enough? Me! So believe me, darling, whatever you're going through, draw the line and pick yourself up! I cried that one last time and decided I would change my reality and believe me, I sure did!

So this all happened in May/June. In the first half of 2016 I was hitting my lowest in life and it was tough but Allah SWT really does bless you and teach you in a very special way.

Imagine that every company you joined didn't work out, your mental health wasn't the best, finances were very poor, your marriage had just been saved and you had a beautiful boy (fifteen months at the time) to look after on top of all this.. shit was about to change!

By August we moved into our own place. YES you read that right! In September I joined the company that changed my life and me and it was a product that I totally hated! I fell pregnant in October but unfortunately in November I miscarried and then from there I was just climbing the mountains of Success.

From hitting the company car plan, earning an amazing amount, my husband leaving his job two months into joining, going to Canada, the list goes on! If someone had told me whilst I was on the hospital bed crying that two months later I would be happy and content in my life, I would have laughed!

So trust me, darling, wear your pain like a crown.

After this I had many ups and downs in my journey of success which resulted in leaving my company, trying others and then eighteen months later rejoining and starting from scratch.

Now the reason I share this with you is because I know how frustrating life and business can be, where sometimes you want to just pack up. But imagine going into an exam and not knowing what paper you're sitting (sounds bizarre I know). We get taught in life which then shapes us with the right skills and grows us into the right person to perform for the next chapter.

I have elaborated on a few areas which I think are important when it comes to becoming successful and leading the best life whilst juggling family life, the dark society, mental health and the business shabbang.

Mental health is your core

Would you turn up to work with chicken pox? OF COURSE NOT! So why do we think it's acceptable when it comes to our mental health?

The moment we get hot flushes we always say, "I'm coming down with something," and start medicating ourselves to minimise our symptoms so we recover fast. Why do we not do this with mental health?

I brushed my symptoms under the carpet for months which pushed me into the most horrible dark place. It's something that I talk about openly to help at least one person daily, especially in our Asian community as women are alive but they aren't living!

See with me, it took a lot of courage to even speak about how I was feeling and when I first spoke about it I was laughed at by a family member. Which of course I took to heart even more, hence why I then shut it down. I have had even my dearest in hospital for weeks because of a number of mental health problems and believe me, it's a horrible feeling.

You can't succeed if you're mentally not well. It's a huge statement to make, but with mental health comes low self belief, low confidence, lack of energy, poor decision making and so much more. The vibes of a happy human compared to a mentally stressed human are VERY different and do impact all aspects of life. As they say, you can't fill from an empty cup!

So what to do?

Invest in yourself! I'm not saying go on a four star all inclusive to Dubai (even though that would be ideal, right?), but make time for yourself EVERY SINGLE DAY. Even if it means you run a bath to relax, read a book, meditate or even draw.

Anything is something, trust me! I love editing images, so I do it when I'm stressed and it really helps me. So find your relax point and embrace it. When you give yourself time to breathe... you're letting go of all that worry sitting on your shoulder.

I know Coaches love this method but believe me, it works! JOURNALLING. Journal the crap out of your life, literally! Journal when you're happy, to be grateful! Journal when you're down, burn that crap so you can let go. Journal every time you panic, or your anxiety is triggered, or you're starting to feel depressed so YOU'RE in control and know the factors, people or situations that don't serve your mental health so you can overcome them.

Self-love! How do you expect the world to love you

when you don't? Get some paper and write down ten things you love about yourself, and add to your list daily. And then write down your weak areas. How can you change them into a positive?

With self-love comes self-talk, Have you ever listened to your inner voice? I want you to pay real attention! Have a little notepad and write down your self-talk. You will be surprised! And then ask yourself, would you say the same to your sister? Partner? Parent? OF COURSE NOT! So why is it acceptable for you?

The moment you hear yourself speaking down or negatively to yourself, CLICK YOUR FINGER and stop yourself and reword into a positive.

The list goes on for what you can do and the tasks you can implement in your daily life to strengthen your mental health, but remember that you are in control and you can change it all. If it gets too much, there's plenty of help available around you and even online, but don't ignore your feelings.

Goodbye society!

Well, well, well? See, we live in a society where even smiling becomes a problem. If she's happy in her marriage, it's an issue. If she works away from her kids, it's an issue. If she wears a dress, it's an issue. If she has a takeaway, it's an issue, and so on.So to be honest, you have to outgrow the society. Remember we are dealing with a community and a culture which had rules planted by our grandparents and their parents.

Truth is, you could do everything by the books and you would still be in the wrong because the current people in our society are very narrow minded and judgemental who can't see the positives in situations and instead see the negatives and problems.

So as long as you're passionate about what you do, you have your goals and vision, and you're going towards life happily .. nobody else matters! Adapting this kind of attitude where you are blocking out the society and their "norm" will make it easier for you to succeed in it, otherwise you will be stopping every time a dog barks, as they say.

Business and Babies.

Being a mum of two, handling a home, husband and two businesses isn't a walk in the park and I would be lying if I said it's easy! It's not! But with a plan in place, it's do-able. Even if you don't have children but have a lot on your plate at home whilst working from home, you can still apply the same methods.

Now, quick question! Can you be in two places at once?

OF COURSE NOT! This is where we go wrong. At one time we get so overwhelmed, we wear all the hats at once. Breathe. So I'm going to break it down for you, and would love for you to try it even for a week!

First of all, what is your generic day? Like what happens without fail? Draw a table, having Monday to Sunday and write this down. For example: Brushing your teeth, Posting on Facebook, Sales ad, Coaching session, Picking up the kids, Making food? You get the idea, right? Then add any tasks you need to do, like appointments or 121s etc.

Once you have done this, then identify where you have gaps in your day. Girl, these are your money making gaps! Understand that you can only be wearing one hat at once, so if you're a mum feeding your kids you won't be posting deliveries, right? And accept that.

Once you rule out what needs to be done daily and that actually you still have a few hours of free time, this will make it very easy for you to handle both business and babies. You can then insert power hours into your daily routine where you can get shit done.

I knew I used to have a lot to do but I never used to schedule my days, so daily my anxiety would be high knowing I had so much to do with little time. Once I started becoming more organised I actually realised how much free time I had which I could utilise. This then took away my anxiety. I became more productive in both areas which then resulted in a happier and more content me.

Business shabbang, the tips and tricks!

So how did I manage to see success after joining ten companies, trying sales and services but never losing the courage? Well, the first question I have for you is, DO YOU BELIEVE IN YOURSELF?

I believed in myself so much that I would give my all to every company and if it didn't work in the first ninety days I would move forward (btw I don't teach this now, I was learning back then – lol).

The industry certainly helped and guided me about my vision and goals. I remember sitting there one evening with a whiteboard drawing my ideal life. A house, a Mercedes and two kids with my husband and an income figure.

I was severely depressed so my whiteboard was my motivation and I would look at it and get happy in excitement every single day that it was happening.

But twelve months later it did! I never gave up on my vision as I trusted the path I was on. Success never comes easy, and unfortunately we live in a world where we have little patience and want everything fast. So draw your ideal life, be detailed and have it in front of you daily! It's coming, darling, trust me!

Think long and hard about your goals, both business and personal. Have your current world around them. Have you ever spoken about someone and then they walked in or called?

That's law of attraction. Use the same principle with your goals and vision! Change your phone wallpaper, daily affirmations and act like you are the person who has achieved all this, because manifestation is key.

So previously I asked you to write your diary out and what you do daily without fail. What money making tasks can you add in to your day that you will do without fail that will push your business to the next level? And then commit to it for at least twenty one days. The results will be huge!

Have one powerful money making hour daily rather than cramming it into one day leaving you with six unsuccessful days. When you master this, your business will be booming daily!

Sales, sales, sales. Stop selling and start helping is what I say. People don't want to be sold to but they want to be helped! Look at your products and ask yourself a question: what solution do my products provide?

Help people to be fit, help people to lose weight, help people's skin conditions, etc. Brainstorm and elaborate. Believe me when I say your product helps a lot more than you think.

A little branding goes a long way. This is my fave part! Do you know pretty little thing by Umar Kayani or by the pink clothing company? Of course, the pink clothing company!

So build your brand in such a way that it makes YOU stand out in those 1000s! Doesn't matter if you're a baker, network marketer, fashionista or even a coach .. BRANDING does everything! From colour scheme, logo, font, images, wording, ads.

It will push your business to a whole new level! I've had clients who have gone from £500 monthly sales to £4000 just by building their brand and targeting their customers accordingly. Little Crystals Company on instagram, check them out!

Don't fake it till you make it, please! It takes a lot for our women in our society and culture to take the leap of faith and work from home, I say that from experience. When you fake results and make it look like a walk in the park, you are giving false hope to a woman who's vulnerable in her situation.

Huge statement, right? We work from home for many reasons: financial issues, goals, needing divert of attention, etc. So telling such women that they will be a high earner instantly or that they won't have to work hard is very dishonest. Be truthful of your journey, how real your field is and the actual possibilities in the correct time frame. People love honesty!

It's a wrap.

Firstly, thank you so much for reading my chapter! Sharing what I have wasn't to gain anything from you but to give back to a woman who's on the same journey! Even if you have taken one tip or point, alhamdulillah x 1000 my job here is done!

I would love to connect with you so we can support one another's journey! Remember life will throw all sorts at you, but that's to prepare and shape you for your next chapter. So embrace it, sister, as your best is yet to come. May Allah shower his success and barkat in your path :)

ASHII AKRAM

Ashii Akram has always had the ultimate passion to help others from when she was young, whether it was a family member or a customer at her retail job. She would always go above and beyond without looking to gain anything in return.

She turned this passion into a mission when she came into the network marketing industry in 2015, and has since been a walking example of how to become successful on social media all from the comfort of your home, one of those rags to riches kind of stories but more on the mental health side!

Her journey started in 2015 with the goal of helping others, and she has proven that time and time again.

A successful entrepreneur who is the CEO and founder of Crystalpreneaurs, where she opened one platform that branches out into different areas to help as many as she can.

Her mission has always been to lead by example becoming a voice of many.

She became a power rocket in 2016 when she went from a hospital bed to a four figure weekly earner within months.

Her quick success in her current company gave her the opportunity to travel to Canada to be recognised. Her story also gave her the opportunity to have an interview with GEO news and was aired nationally. Hitting such a prestige rank with such a small team, she's an example of coaching others to their success, some of whom are now in other companies leading the UK team which is phenomenal.

Despite being a full-time network marketer, she also has a

fashion based direct-selling organisation with the same wholesaler as Missy Empire and Rebellious Fashion. She saw a gap in the market and allowed women to work from home selling a range of clothing from modest Asian wear to western English wear.

And that isn't all. Ashii also qualified as a NLP Practitioner in 2018 which she performs with passion. She opened a platform which enabled women to anonymously share their problems and they would get help and guidance through open feedback.

A mum of two from Manchester who has it all going for her, she's passionate about everything she does and loves every second of it. Her mission is to help as many women as she can mentally, physically and financially and if you follow her on snapchat you can see the dedication in her work daily.

Contact:
Website:
www.crystalpreneaurs.co.uk
www.signaturecollectives.co.uk

Email:
info@crystalpreneaurs.co.uk

facebook.com/ashiiakram

instagram.com/ashiixakram

snapchat.com/add/ashayyxox

6

FINDING YOUR TRUE PURPOSE

*I*n the name of Allah - Al-Fattah - The supreme solver, The opener, The reliever,

The judge, The one who opens for His slaves the closed worldly and religious matters.

Thank you for taking the time to read my chapter. I hope you can take something beneficial away from my reflections and new learnings.

In the recent years of my life I started a journey of finding my true purpose in life. It required some deep internal work and a great journey of healing. Through prayer, patience and a newly discovered higher purpose to serve humanity I found peace and contentment.

The truth is that everyone has a true purpose which is often layered with learned behaviour.

Let me ask you, do you ever feel like you don't fit in and you go out of your way to try and be like those around you, so you appear to be 'normal'?

Have you ever found yourself questioning if there is a greater purpose?

These are some of the questions I often asked myself that left me feeling confused. I knew that I hadn't discovered my true purpose until only a couple of years ago. Being a Muslim, I knew why God created mankind and what my role was as a Muslim, yet I was eager for my personal evolution.

Knowing who you are comes with connecting your mind and the soul, as the true essence of the human being is found when the soul is nourished, and the mind is taken care of.

Your soul craves God and knows the truth. It has the answers to all of your questions if you are open to understanding them. God has created the soul and the ego and to be the undoubtedly successful woman that you are, one needs to be nourished and the other broken. Think about it: which one are you feeding?

Whenever someone asked me about my passion or what I wanted to do in life, I had some ideas and some things that I really wanted to achieve. Other than that, I felt really confused as to what my deeper meaning of life was about.

Growing up in a family of seven children, we had lots of fun and memorable times, yet learning and practising the religion was also encouraged greatly. I remember from a very young age I used to memorise surahs of the Quran with my siblings and had to prepare to be tested by our father every Wednesday.

We took great care in our recitation and took it very seriously. I'll never forget the feeling of being next to recite, although I was mainly excited because I knew I was the best reciter out of us all! I will always give credit to my father for making me a lover of reciting the Quran.

I used to contemplate on the meanings and what I understood of them. My mother has taught me how to remain strong and to do what's right by me. She always told me to focus on my heart more than my appearance and that will remain with me forever.

All of my siblings have a special place in my heart as they represent different forms of goodness in my life, especially my eldest brother, who's always guided me to achieve my goals and focus on happiness.

All I knew was that I had a great love for my religion, and I knew in my heart that I wanted to do something great in life where I could share my love for my religion and serve people too. I couldn't at that point figure out how I would do this.

It is only now that I understand my true purpose and have combined my religion into my work making women stronger in their deen and in their mindset. All praise be to God!

I was always taught to give and give a lot. I was taught to forgive and overlook other people's shortcomings. One thing that I didn't do was to strike a balance. I often gave to a point that I didn't consider my own needs.

I often 'forgave' people too quickly and then later understood what had really happened, the patterns I kept noticing in my life, leaving me full of anger and resentment!

Sometimes I felt like I didn't know who I was fully, and I always knew there was more. I used to feel other people's feelings and literally absorb their problems and take on their pain. I have always been an empath. Sometimes it's a great quality to have and at other times it's not! It's all about balance.

Life and its challenges really tested me throughout my teenage years. I had hopes and dreams, but something was stopping me from feeling motivated or inspired. I felt even more lost and confused when my parents split up.

After that point I let my emotions take over and found my thoughts spiralling out of control. Life goes on as it does, and things seemed to get worse because of the energy and thoughts I was carrying but at the time I did not know this.

I accepted life for what it was and put everything down to the will of Allah. I went through life with a victim, suffering and accepting mindset. I always valued others over myself and always put others first.

After a number of years, becoming a mum to three beautiful children and allowing myself to tolerate so many things that were unacceptable, I found myself in a dark hole of depression and anxiety.

The hole seemed to get bigger and darker as the days went by. I used to question myself, 'Am I not a good Muslim? Am I a bad person, and that's why I'm feeling the way I am?' I just wanted answers and a reason to feel the way I was.

I knew in my heart that I loved a little too much and felt a little too much when I didn't have to, which always put me into situations where I put others first even if it meant putting myself in danger! I lost enjoyment in life and thought, this is it.

This is my life; this is what Allah has willed for me, until one day I sat in a dark room alone and I knew enough was enough. I was tired of the panic attacks and the ongoing feelings of loneliness and deep sadness, the fear and the hurt.

I asked Allah, 'Oh, Allah, please take me out of this dark hole and show me light.' As I said this, I remembered an Ayah from the Quran where Allah tells us that He will not change the circumstances of a believer until he changes himself. At that point, I knew I had to do something and receive professional help. That's when my journey of Healing began.

I received coaching and ongoing therapy from amazing professionals. It was time to dig deep and let go of all the trapped emotions and memories that stopped me from being my true self. I peeled through myself like the layers of an onion until I found just me and my true being.

It was only then I could really learn about myself and love myself. Through this journey I found my true purpose in life, the missing piece to complete the puzzle I had often questioned. I worked on myself day in and day out until I learnt so much about myself that I was able to see my higher purpose in life.

I realised I had a lot to offer the world and I was not going to stop until I was able to spread my message to as many women as possible! The biggest lesson I learnt was to control the mind before it controls and you and to master your emotions before they become the master of you! Everything else just fell into place.

I regained self-belief, self-love and worth and have imprinted in my mind that anything is possible, and I will not stop until I achieve my goals. All with the help of Allah, almighty. I realised how blessed I really was and how Loving my creator is! One thing that really used to bother me was when people would say, 'Depression comes from neglecting your prayers and distance from God.'

Now I'm not saying that's not PARTIALLY true, but who really wants to hear that when they are the worst point in their life? Let's just take a moment to understand what depression and anxiety really are. Depression is a form of deep sadness which stems from holding on to the past, and anxiety is a fear of the future which could also be linked to past experiences.

There are many people who pray, yet they are feeling depressed and that does not make them a less of a Muslim! I noticed that in the Pakistani and Muslim community there was a lack of support and talk regarding mental health.

Even in the mainstream media, everything is based on how we should look physically. I must admit I fell into that trap too until I changed my mindset and came to learn that everything internal manifests externally. Your outer world is a reflection of your inner world.

Throughout my journey of self-development and healing I found myself connecting to Islam in a way that I never ever did before. I was learning about myself and realised that Allah did not create me or any other human being to play small.

We are on this Earth to love the life we live and serve others throughout our higher purpose. I was reconnecting myself to my Lord and the biggest light bulb moment for me was realising that Islam is self- development!

I started to put together everything I was taught and linked it to the teachings of Islam and the way of our beloved Prophet, peace be upon Him.

Here are some ways in which you can instantly change your state and work towards a positive mindset:

- Wake up early - stay awake after morning prayers and have some time alone.
- Journaling - I use it as a form of contemplating the good I have done and where I need to improve. Hold yourself accountable.
- Gratitude - Gratitude is the best attitude! Allah tells us in the Quran in Surah Ibrahim 'When you are grateful, I will give you more...'

I want you to write at least ten things daily that you are grateful for. Focus on the feelings and not just the words. When a person is in the state of gratitude, it is impossible for them to feel any negative emotion! Try it!

Meditation - Take a few minutes out of your schedule to sit and focus on yourself. Take a few deep breaths in and release. As you do this, let any negative thoughts pass you by and replace them with positive and loving thoughts!

If you make these things part of your daily routine, you will feel a shift in your emotional state and in your mindset too.

Since then I have transformed my mindset and went on to achieve many of my goals. I have been working with women to remove their limiting beliefs, remove deep rooted negative emotions and to create a positive mindset so they can find their true purpose in life.

Here are some amazing facts about the unconscious mind so you can understand how powerful it really is:

- The unconscious mind stores memories and organises them, it even represses memories with unresolved negative emotion for protection.
- The unconscious mind preserves and runs the body.
- Is a highly moral being.

Takes everything personally - you will become whatever you tell yourself. Feed your mind with positive words. Positive affirmations are a great thing to practise every morning.

Presents repressed memories for solution - this is when you know it's time to heal and move on.

Is the domain of the emotions - to master your emotions you need to work on your mindset until the unconscious and the conscious mind merge to give you a powerful mindset.

Maintains instincts - have you ever ignored that gut

feeling and then regretted it later, yes so have I! Always listen to your instincts!

HOW TO FIND YOUR TRUE PURPOSE

I want to share some tips with you on how to find your true purpose:

Write down all of your limiting beliefs - become aware of them and work on replacing them with beliefs that will serve you.

Work on shifting your mindset - daily gratitude, affirmations and journaling will give you a great head start.

Invest in yourself - Get yourself a coach! A coach will help you turn your doubts into strengths and will guide you on your new path. Be open minded - know that nothing is impossible. Aim high!

Write a list of things that you've always wanted to achieve and see what those things have in common.

Ask yourself - What can I offer to the world?

If you are easily affected by other people's energy, it is so important to protect your personal space. I am going to share some ways in which you can protect your energetic field:

Avoid negative people - these are the people who love engaging in gossip and find problems to every solution!

Be mindful of what you watch on the TV/media. Practise meditation regularly.

Connect with nature and release negative energies.

Spend time with people who are positive and open minded.

Speak with those who want to see you grow - you will be like those who you choose as your company.

Understand other people before reacting. When we understand why a person behaves the way they do based on their programming and resources it's easier to forgive and move on.

ALWAYS BE YOU

Remember that being you is the best that you can do. No one can be like you so don't try and fit in or go out of your way to be like others. You have your very own qualities and your own personality that no one can take away from you.

Live your life using your qualities to make a difference to those around you. Always remember that you were not created to be miserable or sad. Let go of the victim mentality and up your game!

PERCEPTION IS PROJECTION

You will always see in others what you are feeling yourself. If you do not heal from the past and let go of what doesn't help you become a better person, you will always project it onto others.

The same goes for what people say about you. They will only see in you a reality of themselves. This is something important to think about!

BE AT CAUSE NOT EFFECT

Being at cause is taking responsibility for everything that happens in your life. Even if there are things that happened in your life that were not pleasant, think about what could have been done to avoid it? And what can you learn from those situations, take those learnings and remember them for the future!

Being at effect is blaming everything and everyone for the things that happened in your life. It is the victim mindset that does not help you grow as a person. Life is full of lessons and tests. Choose to see the good in them all and move on!

Finally, I want to share with you some valuable lessons I have learnt:

Anything is possible if you believe in yourself. Without loving yourself you can't expect to be loved or love others truly.

The opinion of other people is not your truth. Anything worth having is worth working hard for.

You must be your number one priority. If you don't take care of your mental and physical well-being you won't be taking care of anyone effectively. It's okay not to feel okay sometimes - have a moment and then get back up. Don't allow yourself to stay down for long. Embrace the feelings and find the solutions.

There is nothing you can't learn. Make the intention, be dedicated and see results!

The best thing a person can do is to invest in themselves - their mental and physical well-being. Master your mind and you will master your body! Aim high and work hard to make your goals a reality.

Choose happiness and joy over everything. Set your intention for the day. Tell yourself - I choose happiness and joy over all!

I hope you enjoyed reading my chapter. If you take away

even one thing from this and implement into your life. That is a form of success from me!

> "Amazing is the affair of the believer, verily all of his affair is good, and this is not for no one except the believer. If something of good/happiness befalls him he is grateful and that is good for him. If something of harm befalls him he is patient and that is good for him"

(Saheeh Muslim #2999)

At the age of eighteen, I learnt this hadith and only now at the age of thirty do I understand what it means. How amazing is the affair of the believer that our main role is to express gratitude and find peace in every situation.

There are so many things now that I understand as my wiser, more empowered self that I learnt at a younger age but never truly experienced.

Sending waves of love and peace to you amazing women reading this! Go and find your true purpose. x

Noshiela Maqsood

I dedicate my chapter to my wonderful daughter Khadijah-Noor (aged 5). One day you will read this and know how much I love you and how much you coming into my life changed my world. I believe in my heart, that Allah sent you to me to save me from a big trial and as a bundle of love and hope that helped me so much. Always remember that you are special, unique and full of light. A light that the world needs.

NOSHIELA MAQSOOD

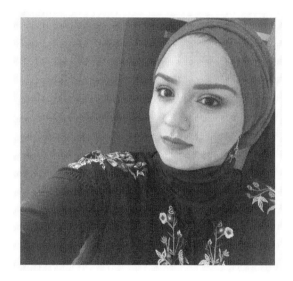

Noshiela Maqsood is a mindset coach.

She takes women through a beautiful journey of healing by focusing on mastering emotions and finding true purpose.

She is passionate about sharing her story and how her journey lead her to where she is, in the hope of inspiring others to make the change they need to improve their lives.

She has always been passionate about helping and serving others and now it's all come together in a holistic way.

Noshiela is a certified Neuro Linguistic Programming & master practitioner.

She helps women to transform their mindset and master their emotions.

She has spoken about her work on BBC RADIO DERBY, Radio Ikhlas and has also appeared on Islam channel (Urdu) and Takbeer T.V sharing her message of women empowerment and finding true purpose.

She is on a mission to change the lives of many through her coaching programmes and workshops. Her passion shines through for all to see.

Contact:

Email:
noshielanoorcoaching@gmail.com
Facebook Group:
https://www.facebook.com/groups/1029110910583276/

LinkedIn:

https://www.linkedin.com/in/noshiela-maqsood-6a4b3b189

facebook.com/NoshielaNoor

instagram.com/Noshiela.Noor

7

WHO DO YOU THINK YOU ARE?

I always thought I was not very confident. I can remember from a young age, one of my teachers expressing her concern to my father - "she is extremely bright but she never raises her hand".

My father, as encouraging as always, would go home and have a chat with me. "Don't be shy," he would say. "If you know something, raise your hand and make sure you participate."

It was only recently I discovered how my father has contributed significantly to my confidence throughout my life. He has always been an encourager, a cheerleader but it was always very subtle. He wasn't particularly explicit but at the same time I always felt it was there. He didn't have the opportunities we had.

Coming to the UK at a tender young age he started work as soon as possible to support his family. He got married to my mother and was soon enough supporting his own children and wife as well as his entire family. He never once let me feel like I couldn't do anything.

He still is a firm believer in education and opportunity, and regardless of the lack of confidence I've always seemed to have in myself, my greatest encouragers have been my own immediate family. I truly appreciate how blessed I am to have that.

My siblings and my parents have always been amazing. Looking back now, I can say I had an extremely happy childhood given the difficulties my parents went through. I never felt without and I always felt loved.

My mother has always been chronically ill since I can remember. She became unwell when I was quite young. My first memory of her being ill was around the age of eight or nine. It was then I began to realise how much of an empath I was – even if it was subconsciously.

In this situation it was fine – I empathised with the stresses my father had to deal with in balancing work, his children and the continuous trips to the hospitals whenever my mother's condition flared up. She finally got diagnosed and it was going to affect her long term, which meant ultimately it affected us all.

Still, to keep her spirits up we were always by her side one by one, whoever was available that evening, and I am grateful to say that being of service to my parents has been my greatest blessing to date.

By the grace of Allah my father encouraged me to go to University. My confidence and self-esteem grew. I secured employment in the top pharmaceutical company in the world and it was a stone's throw away from home. I felt truly blessed.

It was when I went out into the big world by myself, that my experiences began to shape my confidence and lack of self-worth. You will notice I state MY lack of self-worth, because ultimately this came down to me. Whilst certain situations brought out other people's lack of my worth in their life it came down to my own lack of self-worth that ultimately broke me.

I would love to fill you with a sob story of events and people who wronged me but actually whilst life happened (as it tends to) I felt myself spiraling out of control – life kept happening and my self-esteem was at an all-time low. No matter how much my close circle told me how amazing they thought I was – I didn't see it in myself.I digress. When finally my life changed, I was not receiving the encouragement and consistent feeling of worthiness that I had always been given and my life changed very quickly. I had two children and looking back now I can almost certainly say the turn of events around the arrival of my first born, I was a shell of myself.

As a lot of mothers will relate, I had to give up work and become a stay at home mum (something I wanted to do more than anything in the world, to be with my baby). My life turned upside down as I gave up work but at the same time I was torn. I had worked since the age of sixteen and for the first time I had to stay at home, and it wasn't my parents' home.

I felt a bit lost. I all of a sudden found myself experiencing my first dose of lack of self-worth. Many ladies will relate to the constant criticism of having your first child and everything you do questioned and compared to so many others. It's not something just Muslim women will relate to.

It's a little sad to admit but Facebook became my life line. I had not connected with a lot of mums locally as I was working, so instead I connected with people online. I look back now and think I am so grateful – the manygroups I joined with new mamas from all walks of life and they were experiencing the same hardships and difficulties, the constant criticism and comparisons. It is rife in our society and it is a disease.

It was a time when I was becoming frustrated, constantly searching to prove myself in other ways as a woman, as an independent Muslim woman that I could have it all and I would. I was desperate to have an identity which was not related to my children and my husband – an identity of my own. For so long I had been a research scientist. Now what would I be?

I have entrepreneurial blood, I am sure of it – having several businesses from the age of twenty two, I was passionate to stay at home and run a business from home around my kids – If Khadijah (may Allah be pleased with her), the Prophet Muhammad's (peace and blessings be upon him) wife could do it then I was sure I could. She was always my role model.

She proposed to the Prophet (may peace and blessings be upon him) and she was a successful businesswoman and twenty years his senior. I was spiritually connected and my faith has always led me so I was sure it would lead me where I needed to be now.It was at this time I was running an online modest clothing boutique. I had also qualified as a makeup artist just before leaving work for maternity and I was trying to fit that work in on the weekends when someone could look after the baby (no easy feat when breast-feeding!).

Out of the blue one day, when things were really frustrating me, all of a sudden I connected with this beautiful young lady – Uzma, who introduced me to a business opportunity in Network Marketing. She was young and successful, and she had everything I had aspired to and she was ten years younger than me!

It was a post about the car she had qualified for that piqued my interest! I am so grateful that she shared that post. I remember her saying that she was reluctant in sharing the post as she did not want to look like she was bragging.

It was the beginning of a beautiful friendship. I procrastinated for two weeks before signing up and before I knew it I was earning an income from home around my now two gorgeous boys. I was living the dream; I was working from home around my babies and had my own income in a business I was super passionate about.But no matter how much I was praised for my hard work and success I lacked seeing it myself. It was through Network Marketing I discovered personal development work. Since then my life has never been the same.

My business went through ups and downs as I consistently battled with my own nafs ego. My confidence grew as I started to build a team and began presenting live videos on my social media outlets – something I was terrified to do for months.

All of a sudden this new found confidence began to grow. It felt familiar and yet different. I had to encourage myself. My father was no longer constantly around me and my mother's health was quite bad this year which meant he was very occupied with her – I felt bad for constantly needing him to tell me I could do it (even though both Mum and Dad did anyway!).

They say events are really powerful in Network Marketing companies and I can see why. Seeing all the success stories and what people had battled with, really started to resonate with me and I began to emotionally connect to my goals.

When I first started I didn't even know what my goals were. It had been so long since I had thought about what Iwanted. I felt almost selfish for wanting anything for myself.

It was through this journey I found that I had let so many events from my past shape my present and if I didn't do something about it now I was going to ruin my future. I couldn't allow that. I had to be amazing for my boys. They were my why. They still are.

I came across a business coach, Naz, whom I started to work with. She was amazing too – I suddenly began to notice how I was beginning to connect with some amazing women who had been through awfully traumatic experiences and still succeeded. This strengthened my belief that I could do this; I just had this constant ongoing battle with myself, this little voice in my head telling me I couldn't do it. It was exhausting.

Something had to change. My mindset needed work and my lack of consistency was giving me bursts of energy and then nothing at all. I would self-sabotage in ways that were not obvious to me at that time but are crystal clear to me now. Why is that? Because all these amazing women that had got through it had one thing in common — personal development and coaching.

I watched a close friend of mine completely transform with coaching. I was in awe — she had been through so much. How did this happen?

I reconnected with Naz who had now focused on coaching women through emotional mastery. Uzma had launched her Mindset Coaching business and I was full speed ahead.

With some extremely surprising turns of events I finally figured out what I needed to get rid of my lack of self-worth and lack of self-esteem. With both these amazing supporters combined I finally managed to break free from holding myself back.

It's easy to play the blame game — especially when you are in the self-sabotage mindset, thinking that the whole world is against you, but actually it is Allah who reminds us in the Quran, "If you are grateful, I will give you more". It's so easy to become ungrateful when you feel like life is happening to you and not for you.

I decided to relaunch my businesses and train in coaching too, using a number of therapies that helped me and then some. Alhamdulillah these women changed my life, and if I have the opportunity to impact just one woman's life with my message then I will feel like I have contributed to saving one person from going through a similar downward spiral of lack of self-worth and lack of self-esteem as myself. It will literally mean the world to me. But that's not my goal; it's much bigger.

There's a saying that goes, 'women are half of society and they raise the other half of society'. It's so important to have strong, resilient women who do not constantly beat themselves up for being human...for feeling things, for experiencing things. However, it is tough when those emotions take over and you can no longer see the light at the end of the tunnel. Being on a constant emotional roller coaster is draining, and until I was able to work on myself and actually find Coaching and Time Line Therapy with my constant belief in Allah to change everything for me, I really do believe I would still be on that emotional roller coaster today.

I am a firm believer that Allah (you may call it the universe) sends people to you at the right time and I believe every page in my story has been written by the greatest author.

If I had not had those experiences I would not be the person I am today. Do I regret them? Not for a second. It led me to this place and it's a place I am truly grateful for every day. I realised that Allah kept me very protected and averse to things for a long time and only showed me things when I was ready to deal with them.

When these amazing coaches were present in my life, I was ready to make a change, not only for my own future but for women everywhere.

I have found my tribe and I am about to launch my first coaching programme. I am so excited to be helping women and it absolutely makes me jump out of bed every morning to serve the ladies of our society.

A content mother, wife, daughter really does make for a happy home. It also helps us from passing down traumas generation after generation. The buck stops with me.

The amazing thing I discovered about coaching, is how it can completely turn your life around, just from changing the way you think. We become very conditioned in culture but actually Islam encourages self-development.

Coaching breaks all the barriers of culture and yet maintains your dignity because you show up as your best self. You are not bitter; you are kind. You are not sad; you are content. You are no longer fearful — courage becomes your crown.

I feel so truly blessed to be Muslim because without my faith and the fact I could sit on my prayer mat and cry my heart out when I needed to, I do not believe I would have got through what I did.I encourage you all, if you are finding yourself on an emotional roller coaster, just for a minute be true to yourself and ask yourself why you are not allowing yourself to get off the ride. Ask yourself what will it take to be free of this.

You do not have to. Islam came to break barriers and I ask you, what's stopping you from being your true self, your higher self? The journey of working on yourself is not an easy one but the outcome is the most beautiful thing ever and that's why it's become my lifelong passion to help other women break through.

Confidence. Some girls have it; some girls don't. At least that's what I thought.

I would like to take this opportunity to express my infinite gratitude to my family, especially my parents. Without them, I would not have the grit and resilience I have today.

To my siblings, my loved ones, my closest friends (you know who you are) and to those who listened to me for hours on end, especially my wonderful coach, my gratitude here will never be enough. I appreciate you.

To my husband and my children, the reasons I wore courage as my crown, thank you for always supporting me and giving me a reason to be more than I ever thought I could be, constantly believing in me and encouraging me.

To those who came into my life to teach me the most valuable of lessons, thank you. I am grateful as you helped me to grow the negatives and the positives all taught me something...

And I will never stop growing.

TABASSUM SABIR

Tabassum Sabir is a soul centered coach to women in business, mums and passionate ladies everywhere.

She is owner at Be-you-tiful coaching and mentoring, co-owner at online modest clothing boutique Elaneeq, a certified NLP (neuro-linguistic programming) Practitioner and qualified Life Coach.

She is a Professional Hair and Makeup Artist. Her

makeup work has been advertised in Khush Mag and has also featured on recognised boutique websites such as Geeta Arts, as the featured Hair and Make Up Artist working alongside award-winning photographers in the Asian Wedding Industry.

She is also partnered with a Network Marketing company which she is extremely passionate about and has changed her life, and the life of many others.

She also works as a freelance Social Media Digital Marketer passionate about showing local businesses how to raise their profile with simple and effective strategies.

Tabassum is passionate about sharing her life experiences to make sure other women not just survive but blossom in all areas of their lives.

Her mission is to help women flourish into their best self, using the tools and skills she has learned and developed.

She believes that women are here to serve their higher purpose in life and be fully aligned in what they do so they can be the leaders in their own right whether that be in business or in their personal life, to succeed and Be-you-tiful.

Contact:

Website:

www.tabassumsabir.com

Linkedin:

https://www.linkedin.com/in/tabassumsabir/

facebook.com/tabassum.sabir

twitter.com/tabassumsabir

instagram.com/tabassumssabir

*W*hat is the key to success?

I wish my head had a key to open it. I would get my brain out, give it a good rinse under a tap of cold water and place it back. Then, maybe, I might get rid of all the unnecessary thoughts that occupy it. All of the negative voices in my head that make me feel heavy, weighing me down.

With all of the hats that I wear on this head of mine: a daughter, a sister, a wife, a mother of four, a daughter-in-law, a cook, a cleaner, a driver and a servant of Allah; it is so hard to focus on all of these things.

Sometimes I wishfully think, "if only there were ten of me," so that I could try to be the best in all of these job roles. But there isn't, there's just the one Tanya.

Then I ask myself, "If only there were more hours in a day to complete all of these tasks." Yet we only have the twenty four hours of a day that Allah has granted us. So how do I cope? How do I achieve and be successful, and what about looking after myself and my own needs?

That's when my thoughts lingered again, when I felt like I couldn't handle it anymore. And I'd ask myself, "is this my life? Is this what I will do every single day? Wake up, eat, cook, sleep and repeat..." I would console myself with words such as, "It will get easier; just have patience."

That's how I got through twelve years of married life: I was patient. I bore through the drastic transition from being a daughter to a daughter-in-law. Unmarried to having a partner. The burden of responsibility going from singlehood to motherhood.

All of these changes required the utmost patience and that's how I coped. I felt like if I could just turn to Allah through the difficult times then life would get easier. As Allah uses the term Sabr in Arabic.

I used Sabr to get through these different stages but there was still a part of me that I knew could do more. Surely there's more. I needed more. I felt I had so much more to give. I felt like the candle burning in me was at the end of its wick. I needed to reignite it. I needed some passion in my life.

I consulted my Arabic class teacher and she said, "You already have so much on your plate! Focus on your studies!" Although she was right, it didn't stop me yearning for my escapism from my reality.

My mum would say, "Use your degree and look for a part- time job," but the flexibility of a 'job' proved to be difficult as I didn't want to compromise on my children's time. I still wanted to be able to take the kids to school and back or attend their assemblies/parents evenings.

The clock ticks away and time is something that creeps up on you; you can't turn it back, slow it down or freeze it. My children were growing up so fast. I didn't want to miss out on anything. I can't believe I actually have a ten year old that has bigger feet than me!

Some people told me, "Why don't you just wait until they get older?" The question was, how much older? Being a mother doesn't ever end and neither do the children stop needing you, so when does the wait end?

"Have another baby?" an expecting friend suggested. I deliberated for a second and nodded in agreement. That's what I needed. I needed another baby, but not just any baby. I needed a business that I could call my own.I needed to start something, something I could nurture and develop. Something that I was passionate about and that I could bring to life. "Allah (swt) does not burden a soul with more than it can bear" (Surah Baqarah verse 286).

I knew I could do more. I wanted to challenge myself. But with what kind of business? That was the question. I thought and thought and thought about the things I was good at, the things that I enjoy.

One evening, staring at the ceiling whilst breast feeding my fourth child, I saw nail marks from when my in laws had hammered the ceiling whilst decorating mine and my husband's bed for the wedding night.

My memories of our first night came flooding back; the goosebumps of being next to my companion for life. I just thought how nerve wracking and exciting that time really was. I thought how much nicer it would have been if a more romantic atmosphere had been created, with candles and petals, décor that had ambience. That's when I had a light bulb moment.

What if I was the one to create those special memories for newlyweds? I already had experience decorating beds using a hammer, nails and staple gun. Everyone who saw it told me how good it looked and that I should do it professionally… but I never took it seriously.

What if this time I would? What if I used my own experience and knowledge to decorate the room so that the bride felt welcome in her new home?

That memory would be so powerful it would never be forgotten! I didn't know how I would take it to the next level but that's when I made the decision. That's what I wanted to do. I would start my very own bedroom décor business. Suddenly I felt my heart flutter. That candle sparked inside me again, ready to go.

But it wasn't long before that fire quickly burnt out. I'd started researching into all the possible ways of starting my company and became overwhelmed with the voices in my head telling me: "You're being silly."

"You're wasting your time." "What if people don't like it?" "What if you fail?"

"How would you manage the cooking and cleaning and the kids?" "What would people think of you? It's not very respectable."

Self-doubt had crept in and those voices wouldn't stop. That's when I needed the key; that's when I needed those enthusiastic thoughts again. My head felt heavy and my shoulders slumped. So, I reminded myself "have Sabr T, be patient", as Allah reminds us in the Quran 99 times that whenever you feel down, have Sabr.

So, I continued on with my normal life; going out with my husband like I usually do during the weekend. I remember walking through the home section in one of my favourite stores. I was browsing through the décor items, glancing at the glass ornaments and imagining how beautiful they would look in the bedroom.

My eyes gazed at the peonies that would look stunning in a peach themed room. I picked them up to put them in the trolley but looked at the price and put them back on the shelf. My husband caught me staring back at them. I really wanted those flowers. That's when he held me by the shoulder with a stern look on his face.

I remember his words distinctly. "T, don't be scared. I know you can do this. You are amazing at it and you will just get better. I will support you every step of the way. Get what you need and don't look back."

That was all I needed, his reassurance and encouragement. I was worried that my hesitance was holding me back, but I knew I needed to push past my fear and have some courage for once in my life.

I realised I wasn't in this alone and not only would my husband support and encourage me but Allah will always be there to guide me too. I needed to ignore those negative voices in my head and listen to the positive ones.

I needed to find the courage to believe in myself, not undermine my capabilities but positively reinforce them. I reminded myself constantly, if things go wrong have Sabr as Allah never said the road would be easy, but he said, "I will be with those who have patience." (16:127)

So, I went for it. I put all of the items I needed to create my business in the trolley and didn't hold back. I was in love with everything associated with it, from my diary to the cushions. I was captivated with different designs, colours and ideas that I had and couldn't stop myself smiling. That was my retail therapy at its finest for sure.

When I got home, I didn't waste any time. Enthusiastically, I started practising my designs. At the time, this was my and my husband's little secret. I didn't want anyone to know about it just yet. I didn't want anyone to knock me or my idea down before I had even started. I practised arranging the flowers, I played with colours, and figured out ways to store my items in a practical way.

I never thought I'd ever complete a look or that I would get to a stage where I would be satisfied, yet I patientlyplodded along, constantly evaluating how I could do things better. Finally, I felt eager to share my new venture with the rest of the family.

Their reactions were amazing as they were so impressed with what I had created. When they saw my bedroom and my design they were blown away. They had never seen anything like it! That was the reaction I needed.

And that's when my baby was born! We named her just like we had named all of our daughters, with me and my husband just staring at the ceiling canopy of one of my creations. With twinkling fairy lights dazzling over us, we both agreed that it looked so serene, and that was her name: "Serenity Décor".

I didn't even need to brainstorm other possible names, I just fell in love with this one. The next steps involved utilising everyone I knew. Using their expertise to help me develop.

My niece followed my vision through and created my logo, website and business cards. My photographer and staff were selected, and a friend gave me permission to do a photoshoot in her house. My images were taken, and I was ready to go.

Bismillah. My website went live. My Instagram account was activated. Within minutes I received likes from people I did not know. Then a notification popped up. Wait. Did a well-known blogger start following me? I couldn't believe what was happening. Everything was coming together.

Someone commented under one of the images, "Hi, I have just DM'd you." 'DM' what is that? I learnt a whole new jargon. I learnt how to edit my images. I quickly understood how to use the Instagram app and the power of a social media business.

Opening up the notification, I saw the direct message, "Hi I love your work; how much would you charge for something like this in Birmingham?" Birmingham? I didn't even think about travelling and that people would want me to go to their houses outside my home city, but the demand was there, and my work was needed. I instantly replied.

So nervous and not used to the sales pitch I tried to hold a conversation. Although it was awkward and totally out of my comfort zone, I asked all the relevant questions and managed to get a sale and a date written down in the diary.

That was it. I was officially a business; clients were expecting me to arrive at their house on the specified dates and expected me to create that magical experience I promised to deliver.

So as the big day was approaching for my first job, panic

started to creep in my head. What if I forget something? What if my car breaks down? What if the family are not pleased?

I put so much pressure on myself, I felt my head was about to explode. I needed that key again. Bags? Packed. Permission from mother-in-law? Sought. Baby? Ready (yes, my three month old baby was going to come with me I had no other choice as she was breast-fed). I didn't want to compromise on giving her what was best for her and I didn't want anyone else to look after her. I believed I would be able to manage it.

My husband came with me to my first job. I needed him more for the moral support. He tried to help but became my punching bag (for verbal abuse). I found myself hurling all sorts of accusations, throwing every blame on him.

"Where are the screws?!"

"Why did you move that?!"

"Where are the flowers? Did you forget to take them out of the car?"

I became so authoritative. The term 'boss lady' comes to mind. The bedroom décor took over three hours to complete. I had to take two breaks to feed the baby. Once

I'd perfected my design, we drew the curtains to create a bigger impact for the big reveal.

Finally, we asked the groom to enter and see my creation for the first time. With excitement, he ran up the stairs and opened the door. His face dropped. I was so anxious. I didn't know what to expect. His eyes gleamed and he smiled from cheek to cheek. I looked at him with hope and he beamed, "It is absolutely amazing!" The groom was in awe. "I wasn't expecting this. It looks so much better in real life!"

Phew! That was a massive relief. I was ecstatic over the response. The hard work had paid off, but we weren't finished just yet. The client had asked me to decorate the staircase, but we were faced with an issue.

Their staircase banister did not look how I imagined to be, making it difficult for us to decorate it. My head was going to explode. "You silly girl, T, you should have asked the client for pictures beforehand. You should have asked for measurements. You can't assume that it will work!" What do I tell the customer now? How do I tell him I won't be able to do the task at hand?"

I remember feeling humiliated in that moment. All of my worst fears came to life. I had no other choice but to swallow the lump in my throat and I explained, "Salim, unfortunately we aren't able to decorate the staircase as they are not what we expected."

He looked at me and said, "That's not a problem at all! Don't worry about it!" and even though I felt a fool, I offered the refund and quickly packed our bags and left. I was so eager to leave and get out of there as quick as I could. As we left in the car and drove off, I burst into tears, feeling so disappointed in myself for letting this happen.

My husband looked at me and said, "T, they were happy customers. He couldn't believe how amazing the décor was. If anything, learn from it, forget it and move on." I did enjoy it. I loved seeing the twinkle in their eyes. I came home and the next day received the most heartfelt message from the bride and groom about how thankful they were for the decor.

We made it so special for them and that we were always welcome in their home! And that was it. That was my first job completed from start to finish. I told myself that was my first job and my last but the thought of never doing this again made me mourn for it like it was something alive and I had just killed it.As extreme as it sounds, that was how empty I felt. I couldn't bear the thought of losing her and that's when I realised, I was Serenity Décor and Serenity Décor was me…

I had to forget about the negatives from this experience, learn from them and look forward to my next buzz. And that's how life continued. I still need to open my head and I still need the key to open it but what I have realised through this process is the fact that I was able to patiently persevere through this journey. And that patience is actually the key.

Sabr has allowed me to follow my vision through. Sabr has given me the strength to pluck up the courage and start my venture. Sabr is how I dealt with my emotions and if I hadn't had Sabr through those testing times then that key would have remained locked and all my thoughts would have stayed in there, like a cauldron bubbling until it explodes, or leading me down a downward spiral called depression.

But I managed to discover this powerful tool; I just needed to keep using it. Maybe one day I won't need the key anymore, but I doubt it... this is life and life is a test of trials and tribulations. The key to my success has always been Sabr. Everyone has their own definitions of success. The definition of success is having an aim and a goal and making those little steps to accomplish and achieve them: that's what I call success. My business was my own success, a journey that I never thought would come to life.

I assumed it would stay in my mind but it ended up becoming a reality, literally a dream come true. Now three years later, my business has become nationwide. We are in a position to sponsor events such as luxury wedding fairs as well as supporting our local community charity events.

Ask yourself the question, what dream do you wish to fulfil? If you have a passion for something, don't listen to the voices in your head that tell you that you're not capable of doing something. Open your mind with the key called Sabr. Extinguish all of the negative thoughts that hold you back and instead ignite that fire in you!

Dedication

For my four daughters. I hope my story inspires you to fulfil your passions in the future and that no matter what problems you have to deal with in life, you will always remember to have Sabr.

TANYA

Whilst studying at Nottingham Trent University, Tanya worked in HR.

After completing her degree achieving BA (Hons) Social Science, Tanya worked for her Local Community Organisation as a Youth Worker.

Her passion has always been to give the youth of today a

vision in life and help them with the struggles they face in society.

During her career break of ten years, she continued to study an Arabic course as well as learn Martial Arts.

She has four daughters and her mission now is to raise them well, to not have self-doubt and become the best version of themselves!

Tanya is the founder of Serenity Décor, a decor company specialising in the bedrooms of newlyweds.

She is a female entrepreneur who found a niche market that she has developed. Her talent has grown from decorating the bedroom to house decor, as well as hotels and venue styling.

Her creativity has reached over 12,000 followers on Instagram. Serenity Décor attracts clients from different faiths and backgrounds.

Her clients consist of insta-famous couples as well as Vloggers.

She travels nationwide to deliver her service and even has international requests.

She uses her platform to sponsor and support charities and fundraising events.

Tanya has a clear vision of her future, and is really excited about her future developments.

She hopes to inspire mothers and young girls from the Muslim community, in a culture where having your own business isn't as respectable as having an 'academic job role', to not hold back, to be confident and to follow your passion.

Always seek the pleasure of Allah whilst doing it.

Contact

Email:

serenitydecor1@gmail.com

Website:

www.serenitydecor.co.uk

instagram.com/serenitydecor

9

SOULY YOU

'Those who look for seashells will find seashells; those who open them will find pearls.'

~ Imam Ghazali ~

After just finishing my morning prayer and whispering to God with the birds at dawn, I wish I could paint on these pages the peace and serenity I'm enveloped in, as I sit here on the edge of the island of Sicily.

Listening to the crashing waves and watching the array of colours from the sunrise amongst the backdrop of the still mountains and the sparkling ocean before me; a beautiful sight I get to wake up to so often, across so many different countries in the world, Alhamdullilah.

It wasn't always this way. The world left me blinded and broken to such blessings, as I spent most of my latter teenage years and early twenties begging and depending on the temporary creation to fulfil me and my voids.

I can easily recall the countless sleepless nights. The constant cries of despair. The times I stood with a knife in my hand, or a bottle of pills, thinking of the fastest and the most painless way to end myself — to end all the pain.

I had woefully lost myself to the world.

It started from being just an inquisitive girl, rebellious to rules and regulations, to a tearaway teenager from an unstable home environment who questioned love, life and belonging, to a broken-hearted young woman from a premature relationship... to a deeper, darker depression, where I resided for years.

Finally, I started to find a little direction in life. I was about to start my teacher training, but this meant living away from home again, leaving me open to the grasps of the worldly life. I will never forget that night. Trembling, I laid out my prayer mat in the middle of the night.

Frightened and scared, I told God that I knew it had been a while, but I needed saving... that I didn't want to go back to that world.

I truly believe it was that night, coupled with months and months of my mother's desperate prayers for me, that changed my life forever that year... and I found Him. Allah. I stopped so many of my ways. My late nights once filled with music and empty crowds were replaced with nights of solitary reflection and prayer. It had begun, the journey back to myself and back to Him.

After that, my salah became unstoppable, my hunger for knowledge of the Deen addictive. I attended countless classes and courses and travelled to numerous countries around the world, where I indulged in Islamic history and architecture from the cities of Istanbul and Marrakech to little villages in Tunisia.

I learnt Arabic and connected back to the words of God, whilst rushing from mosque to mosque through the bustling city streets of Cairo in Egypt, clutching on to the hand of my Arabic teacher reciting back to her the words of the Holy Quran; to Islamic Law and history in the hidden mountains of Andalusia, Spain; to the spiritual teachings of Islam in beautiful Konya, Turkey.

Whilst basking in the beauty and teachings of Islam, Iwas

also blessed to carry out Umrah, the blessed pilgrimage to Mecca, with my whole family. It was yet another answer to a prayer that I truly never thought would get answered. My father was living on the other side of the world, my sisters were still alien to the journey I was on, and my mother who also dreamt of going, thought it was impossible considering the circumstances.

But, on the day of Arafat, just before I opened my fast, tears streaming from my eyes, I sat in front of the TV, watching the thousands of people cloaked in white, raise their hands and pray, and I begged God to allow me to be one of them.

A few months later there I was standing before the holy Kaaba hand in hand with both my parents begging them for their forgiveness for all the pain and worry I had put them through, during my dark troubled years.

It was only then I started to feel I was deserving of a new life and stopped dwelling on my past regrets and mistakes and stood testimony to the fact that if you take a few steps towards Allah, He, the Almighty comes running towards you. He truly answers all prayers.

My religious journey was not without its battles, coming back to the practice of Islam almost like a revert, and seeking knowledge in a world so fragmented and divided in its teachings, left me beyond confused. There were sects and labels everywhere, and I didn't know where I belonged amongst it all, where the truth lay, which teachers, or ways to follow.

But like many who enter Islam or turn back to Allah with so must zest and passion, I wanted to ensure I was adhering to every single thing that I was told. I became quite strict in my practice and living, and shunned away the world, sheltering away aspects of my vibrant personality and dreams, under a false cloak of modesty and piety.

I found myself becoming quite arrogant and judgmental at times with people around me and it took me a while to slowly realise that this was not aligned to my true self and soul. I had been injected with so much fear of God, that I had forgotten to live with the other wing of hope – His Rahmah and Mercy, for myself and others.

The true essence of Islam and true connection to Allah should only serve you to become more compassionate, open-minded, inviting, and drenched in love; for if love was to speak it would only utter God's name.

The outer practice of Islam alone is empty without the inner spiritual connection, and true practice lies in marrying the two together. My journey continued to incorporate more and more of my inner world, soul and heart, until I was stripped away from all labels, teachers and preachers, until all that remained was me and my Lord.

Just a Muslim, who submitted herself to God with nothing but love and light on a peaceful middle path.

One of the most beautiful aspects of Islam is that we believe we were all created and born with a pure fitrah, a natural inner state of love, peace and truth. As we live on in the world so much of that is lost and clouded, and the outside noise drowns out so much of our inner truth, voice and intuition.

Confined in a circle, everywhere we turn we are surrounded by temporal worldly creation. The only way we can truly escape the external circumference of our worldly existence is if we turn inwards, and face our creator, to the centre, to our souls. Only then can we become eternally present with God, by aligning ourselves with our soul's natural state and calling.

Truth and peace truly lie within. We are too busy working from the outside in, whether that's through materialistic living and temporary fulfilments or outward forms and validations. But, once you start working from the inside out, your whole world will change, a world truer to you.Alongside my spiritual journey, my teaching career opened up so much for me. I relish working with children, whose innocence, truth and beauty never fails to bring me so much joy. Children always help to bring out the true essence of who we truly are and bring out the child in us, a child we should always fight to keep alive.

Another big blessing that came out of my teaching, was a trip I took with some fellow teachers, to Sierra Leone, to help build a school out there. It was here that I first witnessed that nothing served my soul more than service itself.

As my eyes gazed upon starving children, destitute mothers and fragile fathers, the hunger for serving humanity became etched in my soul.

There were moments that left me crying uncontrollably in hidden corners. The pleading of a young girl asking me to be her mommy... the unsmiling face of a boy dying of malaria... the untreated epileptic fit a child had, leading to her death. Moments that changed my life forever.

I knew I could no longer go on to live a life without consistently doing something for the forgotten people of the world. I returned and prayed for Allah to open a door for me to actively work for a cause and stumbled upon a small and humble charity called Ethar Relief, helping the forgotten Eritrean refugees in East Africa, where I still volunteer till today.

God has blessed us in so many different ways, and it is a right upon us to use our blessings to serve our loved ones, neighbours and communities. Every single one of us has the capacity, however small, to do something in our week, our month, our year that's of selfless service.

After years of happily teaching and doing charity and community work alongside my main job, something began stirring in my soul, a restless feeling, a feeling that grew stronger and stronger and I could no longer ignore.

I was completely perplexed, as my life was beautiful and surrounded by so many loved ones and meaningful work... but there was an aching emptiness that crept up on me, not just in the silent depths of the night but in the centre of crowds.

Although I tried to plaster over it, as so many of us do, looking for temporary escapism and empty distraction, the true callings of my soul haunted me until I had to face it head-on.

It's never an easy process. You have to visit the dark places within yourself to get to the light, and although I felt petrified, I knew I had to trust what I was feeling and align myself with the truth within. After months of reflection, tears and prayers, I started to realise I was no longer comfortable in my comforts, that my soul was aching for growth.

It's intrinsic in all of us to grow, to push ourselves and to continually stretch and reach to new heights within our inner and outer world. There is no growth in comfort, and they say that when we are not growing, we are as good as dead. I literally felt every ounce of this reality, and it was time for me to grow, challenge myself, and change something.

Change invites fear. It's actually a good indication of growth, and instead of trying to eradicate the fear that lies with growth and change, as Susan Jeffers says, 'feel the fear and do it anyway.'

This time in order to change me, I had to change my environment. I was always a free-spirited adventurous soul, a risk-taker, yet I had been in the same job for eight years, constantly busy juggling my career and community work day in-day out. I had become so attached to my job, my projects, my loved ones, that it had begun to hinder me and who I truly was.

Our Prophet Muhammed (PBUH) said, 'live in this world like a traveller.' And although I travelled a lot, I realised the true meaning of that saying was detachment, to live in the world attached to nothing, relying on no one but God, and to free yourself from the shackles of distractions and dependency.

I decided to face my fear of moving away from all I had acquired and loved and move to a country completely by myself. A country in which I didn't know a single person and truthfully didn't even know existed prior to a little research.

Literally within a week of my decision, I had secured a job in Oman in one of the best schools in the country, teaching English and Drama. It all happened so fast, and everything was falling into place so quickly, I knew it was from Allah.

Although at the time, drenched in anxiety, it felt like the hardest thing I had ever done and I needed a lot of support to follow through with the decision, I knew it was still something I had to do. In this, lay my soul's growth.

The soul is our spiritual home, our compass that directs and guides us to our truth and calling, to who we are and where we should be. We have become so accustomed to temporarily plastering over our feelings of fear, restlessness and discontent in this modern world, that we rarely sit with ourselves long enough to explore what it is we are being beckoned to.No matter how much we try and run away from it, it is in the silence of our soul we hear our truth. Follow the silent callings of your soul. When you feel restless, or something doesn't feel right, don't ignore it. Don't ignore your truth, because no matter how much you keep burying it, it will only resurface again and again.

It's not an easy process. It requires courage, to maybe even realise, 'I don't actually like my job,' 'I'm not actually happy in my marriage,' 'I don't actually fit in with my friend's circle anymore.' Whatever it is, confront it. It may be just something that requires addressing or healing, rather than change all together. It may just be a forgotten talent, dream or desire your soul's yearning for you to connect with again, a calling to realign with your true purpose or passion.

Living alone in Oman taught me so much, for someone who lived such a busy lifestyle, always surrounded by so many people, I was surprised at how much I started to love my own company. I rediscovered so much about myself and found myself doing so much of what I loved as a child.

I was able to be my crazy self again from dancing and singing pretending to be in a music video, to thinking I was an actual mermaid. I found a new appreciation for who I truly was and felt free to explore my identity away from societal norms, conventions and expectations of our environments and communities. Sometimes we need to move away a little and give ourselves that space to ensure we are being true to who we really are.

Having so much time to myself, allowed me to sit with my soul for longer periods of time. I spent long days alone by the ocean, reading, writing and conversing with God, nights of beautiful reflection under the stars on beaches, mountains and deserts.

The stillness and pure beauty of nature connects us back to our natural state like nothing else. As we sit in silence amongst God's beautiful creation, we connect with His magnificence, blessings and truths. It's a must, to find time every week at least, to go for a walk or sit in a park, to nourish our souls surrounded by the natural world.

This time of solitary stillness and reflection also brings you to revisit the broken and buried aspects of yourself, which require healing. Every single person has unhealed wounds that lay within us, from the tests, trials and pains of the world and we need time to address and express these.

Expression is key. Express your truths, feelings and self, whether that's through communication and prayer or the power and beauty of art, through music, dancing, painting, writing… whatever your form of expression, allow yourself to express. Silencing and shackling your truth even for a moment can imprison you for a whole lifetime.

Investing time in yourself will only serve you to live a more serving, purposeful, and fuller life. In my attempt to make up for the lost time of giving, I had spent so many years running around putting others before me, I had forgotten to give to myself, and I truly learnt that the more we serve ourselves, the more we are able to serve out to others, and it never rang truer – Rumi's saying of 'you can't pour from an empty cup.'

Most of all I learnt how to be alone without feeling lonely. Once you have truly mastered being alone and learnt to be with yourself, your thoughts, your truths, you can live a life where everything is not just aching escapism, or attachment and dependency to validate you or make you feel whole. Only then, without expectation, can you purposefully live and love from a place of complete freedom.

Everyone has their attachments rooted in the worldly life, materialistic or other. Mine was always people. My attachments with my loved ones became a lot healthier as I realised that every single person, blessing, goodness we have in the material world is just a means of Allah's love. That no meeting is coincidental and everyone who crosses our path, and everything we go through, comes to give and teach us something.

During that year, people who started off as complete strangers became some of the most amazing people I had ever met, who loved and looked after me like their own.

When God wants to protect you and send you his love and care, it comes in different unexpected forms, and no matter where we are, who we are with, whatever portion of love and care is granted for you, He will reach you. Everything is Him, and once you start seeing Him as the source and not the world itself, is when you break free from the shackles of the outside world. As I experienced what felt like continuous miracles, I truly learnt the true meaning of Tawakkul, to fully let go and trust in God and depend on Him alone and seek for nothing outside of myself.

I was living in a wealthy, peaceful country with beautiful beaches at my doorstep, where it was sunny every single day. I had an easy job I enjoyed, which paid really well; I had a driver and had enough holidays to travel to the most beautiful destinations in the world.

My family and friends came to visit me all the time and I started to make the most beautiful friendships. I could have easily stayed there for as long as I wanted and continued living this life of luxury… but it happened again, that stirring in my soul. This time away from all the busyness and noise of life, I was able to hear and follow the calling a lot faster.

It was time for me to return. What I needed to achieve here was done and any more time felt so selfish for me, as I ached to go back and serve again. I missed serving my parents. I also missed the charity and community work I did, and I yearned to share and spread all I had acquired and learnt with others.

We all have deep inside have a natural yearning to love and serve and no other worldly or materialistic accomplishment comes close to the feeling of purposeful giving. I can tell you there is nothing else like it. It awakens so much in you and we owe it to God, the world and ourselves to do what we were designed to do – to give, share and spread love.

Living abroad, it was easier being my true authentic self, and having the time, space and stillness to acquire soulful living. The true challenge for me was to carry my new learnings and rediscovered self, surrounded by the glare, pressures and expectations of society back here in the UK.It was challenging to say the least, especially as I came back having decided that regardless of the loss of income, I was going to do all the things I truly loved and was passionate about. This meant leaving my teaching career to do more charity work, and helping others reconnect with their true life's purpose in a world that sells nothing but the opposite.

Beyond the worldly clouding and conditioning we need to know, own, and pursue our purposeful passions to find true fulfilment in life. Once we discover who we truly are, and what awakens our souls, we must align it with what we do in our lives and have the confidence and courage to do what we know to be true to us. Even if this means having to do things we are highly uncomfortable with, and here lay my challenge.

Everything I wanted to do required me to be constantly seen, heard and therefore exposed. I've always been a fairly confident person and speaker throughout my life, especially when it meant standing up and giving a voice to something purposeful and meaningful but living in an increasingly materialistic and superficial world made me want to keep a low-profile.

I came back to a world possessed with phones and social media, saturated with suffocating images and ideals of beauty and shallow living. A world that a few of my friends had become a part of and one I didn't ever want to conform to. But, as life had taught me, there is no growth in comfort, so it was something I had to learn to live amongst.

I was also back surrounded by my loved ones, dependencies and comforts and the real test was to carry the learning, and still float through life like a traveller, with healthier attachments. To love freely, serving myself and others in balance with more love to give and receive, which I work to uphold till this day.

Almost as soon as I returned, God began opening all the doors I had pleaded and prayed for during my last few months in Oman. I had asked for opportunities to serve the Ummah and to make me a means of serving others through all that He had blessed me with.

Through what felt like another miracle, I found myself travelling the world as an International Aid Worker, working to help refugees and the poverty-stricken in countries from Bangladesh to Iraq, Lebanon and Jordan and soon enough I was using the very social media platforms I hated, to raise money and awareness.

Although I initially felt anxious using such platforms, through posts, pictures and videos I was able to share the reality of the broken world that was in need of desperate help. My purpose was greater than my fear and that's the beauty of living a life filled with purpose and passion: it transcends all your doubts, fears and insecurities.

I had also spent years dimming my own light, afraid of judgement and perception and scared to overshadow others, so they could shine, but I refused to do that now. It dawned on me that by limiting ourselves, we are actually limiting God. It blows my mind when I think of the true nature of our souls, Allah himself 'breathed His soul into man.' (Quran: 32:9) Allah breathed into us of his own Ruh-Spirit, so our pure souls are belonging to the entity of God himself!

When I think of this, how can I not treasure, love and appreciate my soul and all that I am? How can I not reconnect to the magnificence that resides within myself? It's actually our duty to shine and light the world with all that we are, with our beauty, talents and abilities and in doing so, we encourage and inspire others to do the same. Every single one of us has something beautifully precious and unique to offer the world.

I was therefore done playing small and felt God himself would have held me accountable if I didn't continue living out all I wanted to do and share with the world. This gave birth to Zora Soul Coaching. Zora meaning 'Dawn,' a name I originally used for a book club I had started on my return to the UK, filled with enlightenment, which dawned on us through the beautiful sharing of words and reflections.

I passionately started to coach both women and the youth to rediscover their soulful selves. I had innately been doing this for years, but now as a profession, I began helping others connect back to their authentic selves, as I had done.

In a materialistic, consumerist modern society screaming for you to be like everyone else, we have to fight and hold on to our real selves. Don't let your unique self and soul drown and get lost amongst the noise, voices and whisperings of the outside world. In this world of conformity, we have to courageously be our authentic selves, and that courage is contagious and allows other women to feel free to connect with their true selves too.

To be our true selves means we have to allow ourselves to drop our masks and be vulnerable, to be real and raw. To share our stories, our insecurities, our truths. Our imperfections are not inadequacies, they are our truths, that make us human and in them lies our deeper truthful connections with one another.

The more I'm able to sit with, express and openly share my own insecurities, fears and doubts, the more people I soulfully connect with, and through that beautiful, humanistic real connection there is so much liberating self-discovery, healing and success.

Our true selves are not lost, they are right there buried under our cultural conditioning, self-doubt and limiting beliefs we've acquired from the world around us. Our task is therefore not to find ourselves but to return to ourselves and remember who we were before the world got its hands on us.

The world has become so fearful, guarded and dark, it is crying out for the light of authentic souls. It's not an easy process, and there is no shame in reaching out for help. We invest so much money and time on our outer achievements and successes, but what about our inner world?

As a coach, I act as a mirror, holding up a reflection of your inner world, so you see your buried self, guiding you gently back, but I also need my own mirrors, who also help push me and hold me accountable to living out my truths. No one is perfect: this is what makes us human, and unites us in our truths and struggles, for we are in it together.

You are not just going to read a single chapter, or a book, or any number of books, and miraculously change. I'm going to be honest: it is hard work. It's continuously choosing to work on yourself, and invest in you, to continually dig deep and become aware of your mindset and your hidden wounds, limitations, blockages, truths, darkness and ego, and work through it all and heal.

It is our inner thoughts, feelings and conditioning that affects everything we do in our lives and achieve on the outside. More than any of our external realities, environments and opportunities, it is our internal sabotage and our own created doubts, fears and anxieties that make our perceived failure a reality for us. It is the limiting beliefs we carry, that create or destroy our lives…that empower or poison us.

Becoming awake and aware of our inner realities is therefore vital as our outer world is a mirror image of our world inside. Give yourself time to personally invest in this inner world, which requires you to serve yourself, to be honest and real with your truths, feelings and callings and to seek help when you need it.

We must find time in our everyday lives to continuously connect with ourselves. Even if it's just twenty minutes every morning that you take out just for you, to sit silently away from the world, to bask in gratitude for all that we are and all we have and to spend time soaking in the present moment.

Alongside our prayers, which are designed to do this very same thing, and take us back to ourselves again and again, we must also invest daily in our communication with God, intimately conversing with Him. Invest in spaces that allow for communication and expression, surrounding yourself with true mirrors and spend time with nature and the natural world.

In the modern world where the simplicity of soulful living is so lost, we have to seek out those places for ourselves and in ourselves, to tune ourselves with our truths. You'll find that everything that takes you back to your true natural soulful state, allows you to connect back to God, and everything that connects you to God will take you back to your true self and soul.

Most of all we have to remember we are human, and the world drives us to leave our true self again and again, we are called 'insan' for a reason, which means 'to forget.' I still have my down days, I still have my tests, my insecurities, self-doubts and fears that creep back at times, and so continuously work on myself to stay centred and connected.

Even writing this chapter, I had to fight off reservations of not being worthy enough to share my message, and have come away by myself to a little cottage, in the middle of nowhere, surrounded by beautiful countryside to sit peacefully with myself and continue writing from my heart and soul.

Nothing can exempt you completely from the anxieties, fears, and pains of the world. It doesn't promise you constant ease. The world wasn't designed that way, but when you know throughout life you can reach and connect to something that lies within, and work to realign yourself with your true natural state, anything and everything becomes possible.

It is without question the power that lies within us and our own minds to overcome our struggles and achieve our goals and dreams, but that alone won't sustain you. When you truly connect to the source, the creator of our mind, body and soul then your world will be nothing short of miraculous and your possibilities, dreams and talents will be limitless and endless.

When you live a life for Him, with Him and through Him, you attain true contentment and success. Every single experience and achievement I've been beautifully blessed with, none of it has been possible and will continue to be possible without my connection to Him, my creator.

God guides us within, and whatever we are searching for to attain in this world, we know with whom and where it is that true beauty, love and peace resides, with Him and within us. I pray and hope we all go through this journey in life remembering where we came from, from Allah Himself, how beautiful and precious we all are and to connect and hold on to that truth and let our God gifted souls shine out into the world.

Dedicated to my Creator and to my beautiful parents, without whose love and prayers I'd still be lost to the world and to my inspiriting soul circle, especially my soul sister Sadia, who has lovingly supported me through every step of my journey x

ZOBIA ARIF

Currently living in Birmingham, Zobia is a warm, ambitious and inspirational woman who relishes in the world of travel, art and adventurous living.

Passionate about serving the youth, Zobia provides private tuition, develops and delivers innovative teaching initiatives and offers her counselling experience and skills to various youth mentoring programmes and organisations.

She draws on a decade of secondary school teaching experience, where she taught English and Drama, empowering young people, in some of the most deprived schools in the UK and most privileged schools in the Middle East.

As an inspirational speaker, Zobia also delivers dynamic and gripping speeches, workshops and courses, continuing to empower and inspire young people across the Midlands.

Zobia is a certified Life Coach and NLP (Neuro-Linguistic Programming) Practitioner, and founder of Zora Soul Coaching, where she works with a diverse range of people, deeply connecting them back to their authentic, soulful selves and unearthing and unleashing their true inner potential.

Through motivational speaking and personalised private coaching, Zobia helps women embrace an empowering mindset and overcome their anxieties and limitations; injecting them with courage and confidence to live a truer, purposeful and fulfilling life.

Creating a soulful safe space for young people to share,

express and communicate, Zobia also provides private and tailored youth coaching.

Promoting emotional and mental wellbeing, Zobia helps teenagers and young adults to achieve both their academic and personal life goals with more confidence and meaning.

Working with numerous charity organisations, Zobia regularly travels as an international humanitarian to some of the most impoverished places on earth, delivering lifesaving aid to refugees and those in need.

Living her message, Zobia's purpose and passions have led her to embrace a life of growth, travel and service.

Contact:

Email:

Zobia@ZoraSoulCoaching.com

Website:

http://www.zorasoulcoaching.com/

facebook.com/zobia.arif.9

instagram.com/z.o.b.i.a.a.r.i.f

10

LOVE, SUCCESS AND POSITIVITY

*W*elcome to my chapter. My name is Zulekha. Thank you for taking time out to read my story.

I would like to start off with introducing myself. I am a British Pakistani Muslim woman, a charity fundraiser, a hijab stylist, I work in the wedding industry and I'm also an ambassador for 'world hijab day'.

You might think that's a long list of things I do, but it's everything I enjoy doing and always wanted to do. Charity work has always been on top of my list, helping those in need, making a difference to their lives, putting a smile on their faces. It's what makes me happy the most, but it took time to build that up as a career.

Like many women, I thought my duty was to stay at

home as a housewife. This was due to the cultural background I came from, and I was made to believe it was also a part of my religion, but as time went on I came to learn that I am allowed to go out and work, I can do what I really want to do, and my journey began from there.

When working, I'm not held back from fulfilling my duties towards my family. Many women refrain from working or education because they are told that they don't need to make a career for themselves. They are told to do the household duties and to become a housewife, which, yes, if you are happy with, then that's fine, but if you aren't you do have the right as a Muslim woman to make other choices.

Being a Muslim woman from the Pakistani background, being married with a family, and building a career, has been one of the most challenging tasks I have encountered. I have many rights and I have learnt that building a career was one of them. My religion had been wrongly mixed with the sub-continental culture and this was what I was taught, so I wasn't really sure if I had made the right decision, but I know, now, what my rights are, and doing what made me happy made me who I am today.

Through the years I've had to face a lot of negativity:

fingers being pointed; being talked about how working has got to be affecting my ability to be a good mother, daughter, wife, and daughter-in-law; how I can't be working and still fulfilling my duties in those roles.

However, every time I was put down in life, I've always got up stronger. I've met many negative people in life but I have just as many, if not more, supportive people around me, and I have come to learn that if I want these changes to come about, I have got to implement them first. I have got break free from these cultural norms which hold no place within my religion.

I am a hijabi woman and I love hijab styling. Many women struggle with their hijabs and I wanted to help them out, therefore I took up hijab styling as one of my jobs. By wearing my hijab, I put my faith on display.

Not many appreciated me covering up using a hijab. I was criticised for trying to display perfection when I wasn't perfect, but this was me, an average imperfect person trying to follow the perfect religion, and no one was going to stop me trying.

My value as a human should be defined by my character and not my clothing. I cover up by my own free will, but that doesn't make me any different to any other woman who wants to go out there and make a difference. I shouldn't be put down because of the way I dress, or because of my colour, my race, my height, my weight. I believe I shouldn't be judged or put down for any reason at all. I am who I am and no two people are the same. I am a flower and all flowers in a bouquet are different.

We hold back from teaching our women the importance of being a Muslim woman and the rights we have; we hold back from educating them when "the seeking of knowledge is obligatory for every Muslim" (Al Tirmidhi #74) and letting them build a career.

Khadija (a.s) the wife of Prophet Mohammed was a very successful business woman. My religion allows women to work and it has been done from when it was discovered.

Islam was the first to give a woman her rights and there were many of them. Islam has raised the status of a woman from below the earth so high that heaven lies at her feet.

We are role models for many, from being a daughter to a wife, and then to being a mother herself. Don't let culture take over our religion and ruin your happiness. My religion allows me work and secure a bright future for myself and my family.

I've come across many single and married women, who

have succeeded in their goals and that is all due to self-love and confidence. I have found a lot of the women from the sub-continent suffer due to cultural beliefs but many have broken free from this.

Know your rights as a woman and do what you know is right. You can be the perfect role model spreading love and positivity. If you can keep peace and unity, if you can better other lives through your own, if you can bring a smile to another, if you can make a difference to someone's life through your own, then you have achieved success.

You don't have to be negative because others are. "Do not be around people without minds of their own, meaning that if others treat you well, you will treat them well and that if they do wrong you will do wrong. But (instead) accustom yourselves to do good if people do good and not to do wrong if they do evil" (Tirmidhi).

I believe in being positive in every step in life and most importantly doing what makes you happy. There were times when I had fingers pointed at me because I spoke up for women's rights. No matter what you do people will try putting you down. There are no two people who are the same so not everyone will appreciate you. Someone, somewhere won't be happy with what you do, what you say, what you eat or even what you wear. There will be times where you'll want to just give up, but you have to remember only you can change your own levels of happiness. Only you can make a difference to your own life. Only you can get up after every fall and keep going, and that's when you will become successful.

Being successful doesn't mean you will have millions of dollars in your bank account, or a highly paid job, or a flashy car or even a big house. Being happy is loving yourself and spreading love to those around you, doing all those little things that give you happiness: that's your real success – your happiness.

Keeping positive is key in life. Never give up; never hold back. You will gain strength and confidence through every life experience you have. The most beautiful thing you can do is self-love and the greatest thing you can achieve is confidence.

You need to love yourself and build your confidence with whatever it is you're doing. Get up after every fall and accept that success isn't always gained at the first attempt. You will eventually find success, peace and happiness. You can love others and help others, but you can't help others if you are not willing to help yourself first.

"Allah never changes the conditions of a person unless they strive to change themselves"

(quran 13:11)

Sometimes you desperately want to achieve something in life and only you can make that happen. Get up and go for it and keep going until you have reached your goal.

Never hold yourself back from the fear of failing. At times the failing is what makes you a better person. No matter what your goal is, you will face obstacles. There will always be a challenge you've got to face and the most important thing is how you face them.

Sometimes you will want to run away but running away has never been the solution. Face your problems, face your fears, learn from your journey, whatever it may be.

Only learners become masters. If you learn how to overcome your fears, overcome negativity, overcome hate, overcome anything that stopped you from reaching your goal, then you're a master. To have a better tomorrow you need to start today. Just one decision can change your life for tomorrow.

Life won't always be perfect. Once you overcome one thing, be ready for another, laugh at your own mistakes and enjoy what you do and start enjoying the obstacles. They are all a lesson for you. You can never change the past, but what's coming is in your hands.

"Indeed, what is to come will be better for you then what has gone by"

(quran 94:4)

If you want to make that difference then do it today. Start today. Make a difference to your life by accepting every failure, and know that these failures are only the structures to create a better you. The world is a whole better place when you start seeing things with positivity.

You have just got to wake up in the morning, look in the mirror and believe, "today is my day. I will overcome any negativity that's comes my way." Don't change yourself for others. Let others love you for what and who you are. Don't let culture and negativity get in your way. Remember, only you can make a difference to yourself. If you can't make that change – no one can do it for you.

The decision is yours. You might fear the outcome of things so much so that you don't end up doing them at all. If you believe what you are doing is right and you really want to do it, but are scared of the outcome then you won't know until you have tried. Even if you fail once, get up and try again and then you keep trying, repeatedly, if you have to, to achieve success.

That is what will make you a successful person.

It's not about who I am but what I do in life that defines me. Not every day will be a good day but we have to learn to live it anyway. Not everyone I love will love me back, and not everyone will tell the truth, but I have got to keep that honesty and integrity, because my character is what I am and what I do, not what others want me to be. My choices, my actions, they only define me as a character no one else.

Some people will put me down, but I have got to keep getting up, I have got to keep trying, until I know I have achieved what I want in life. People around me might not like what I do, what I eat, what I wear and might have a totally different career to me, but that's ok, and why?

Because that's them and I am me. I don't have to be the same. My individuality is what makes me special. I can never be happy in life if I am not happy with myself. I am happiest when I am myself and if I stay positive with myself, if I stay positive with what I do, that's when others will appreciate me and that's when I will succeed.

I believe in life that I won't always get everything in one go, I won't always meet people who will like and appreciate me, and I won't always reach every goal in one go, but I have learnt that if I keep patience within myself it gives me the energy to get up after every time I didn't achieve my goal. It makes me stronger and better as a person.I believe every obstacle is a learning curve, so keeping that confidence brings me back to fight for my goals. "Be patient, indeed the best outcome is for the righteous." Keep going and make what seems impossible, possible.

Surround yourself with positive people, be happy for others, and others will eventually be happy for you. I am fortunate to have my life partner, who is understanding and has stuck by me through my choices. We ignore the negativity. Be positive, be happy and spread love.

ZULEKHA BASHIR

Zulekha Bashir is a charity fundraiser, event organiser, a hijab stylist, she works in the wedding industry and is also a UK ambassador for "The world hijab day".

Zulekha is passionate about her work. She's been to Jerusalem, Africa and Pakistan, handing out food and clothes parcels, installing clean water supplies and helping the orphaned/poor children by providing means for education.

She's organised challenges such as climbing Mount Snowdon for charity. She is a fundraiser for many charities and runs charity events to help raise the funds.

Zulekha is always happy to help anyone wishing to do a similar sort of work. She also enjoys hijab styling and holds hijab styling classes.

She aims to make a difference to as many lives as possible, especially to those that are less fortunate.

She aims to become a voice for Muslim women, helping them understand their rights and break the cultural society norms.

Contact

Email:

zulekhabashir@yahoo.com

Instagram:

www.instagram.com/amore_occasions/?hl=en

instagram.com/zulekhas_hijabhouse

26854142R00132

Printed in Great Britain
by Amazon